The Munros in Winter is the amazing story of an achievement unparalleled in British mountaineering - the first winter expedition to climb all the Munros in a single journey. Not only did Martin Moran complete the trip, but he also set a new record for the fastest-ever completion of the Munros in any season. Share every moment of the 1,030 miles of walking and skiing, the 410,000ft of ascent and descent, the storms, snows and darkness of winter. Experience the terror of avalanche and of scrambling down a mountain in pitch darkness and a howling gale. Learn of the strenuous physical and mental pressures that were overcome by both Martin and his vital back-up team in this gripping account.

Martin Moran is a British Mountain Guide, and with his wife Joy has run a climbing school in the north-west highlands since 1985. His climbing career developed from boyhood camping trips in the Cheviot Hills to ascents of the North Face of the Eiger and four new routes in the Indian Himalaya. In 1993 he made the first and only continuous traverse of the 75 4,000m peaks of the Alps in 52 days with Simon Jenkins, and since living in Scotland has made over 100 new routes on his local mountains. Joy accompanied him on the Munros expedition, providing the back-up support essential to the success of the trip as well as climbing 120 of the summits herself. She and Martin now have two children, Alex and Hazel.

Martin has always had a special love for the Scottish hills, and this book proves once and for all that *real* mountaineering excitement and challenge can be found in Britain.

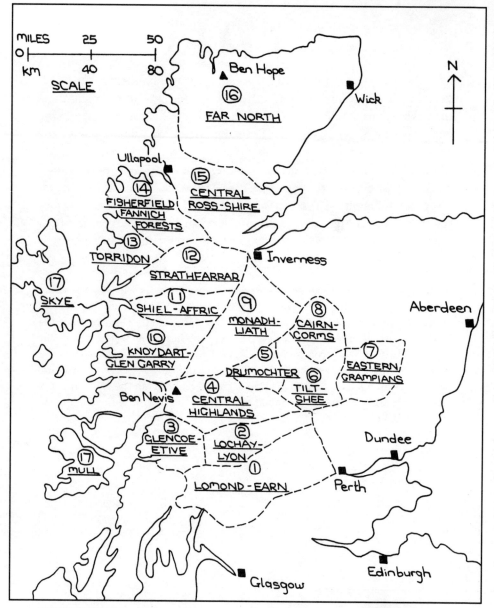

MUNRO'S TABLES: GEOGRAPHICAL SECTIONS (Number of Munros given in brackets)

1 LOMOND – EARN (20)

2 LOCHAY – LYON (25)

3 GLENCOE – ETIVE (23)

4 CENTRAL HIGHLANDS (35)

5 DRUMOCHTER (7)

6 TILT – SHEE (15)

7 EASTERN GRAMPIANS (14)

8 CAIRNGORMS (17)

10 KNOYDART – GLEN GARRY (26)

11 SHIEL – AFFRIC (21)

12 STRATHFARRAR (15)

13 TORRIDON (7)

14 FISHERFIELD – FANNICH FORESTS (19)

15 CENTRAL ROSS-SHIRE (7)

16 FAR NORTH (4)

17 SKYE – MULL (17)

THE
MUNROS
IN WINTER

277 summits in 83 days

MARTIN MORAN

Foreword by Hamish Brown

With best wishes

Martin Moran.

DAVID & CHARLES

MAP SYMBOLS AND CONVERSION TABLES

Key to Map Symbols

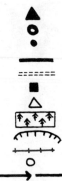

Overnight stopping point/terminus

Munro summit

Munro top or lower mountain summit

Metalled road with public access

Private road or unmetalled motor track

Habitation

Mountain bothy or refuge

Forest area

Major cliff or corrie edge

Railway

Rail station

Line of route

Height and Distance Conversions

(see also Appendix I)

1.6093km	=	1.0000 mile
1km	=	0.6214 mile
1m	=	3.2808ft
300m	=	984.2ft
600m	=	1968.5ft
900m	=	2952.7ft
1200m	=	3937.0ft
914.4m	=	3000.0ft

A DAVID & CHARLES BOOK

ISBN 0-7153-0689-8

First published 1986
Reprinted 1986, 1988, 1991, 1994
New edition in paperback 1997

Printed in Great Britain
by Butler & Tanner Limited, Frome
for David & Charles
Brunel House   Newton Abbot   Devon

CONTENTS

AUTHOR'S PREFACE TO PAPERBACK EDITION

With the hindsight of twelve years as a Mountain Guide and well over 1,000 subsequent Munro ascents, it is a strange feeling to look back on our winter round of the Scottish peaks in 1984–5 and to reread this account of our journey. I am at once struck by the enthusiasm and innocence with which Joy and I abandoned our careers and set forth into the wilderness, the pleasure and satisfaction with which we traversed each group of hills, and the immense gratitude we felt for each fine day and each icy sunset. Long and occasionally harrowing experience, coupled with an increasing familiarity with the hills in their varied moods, can easily let us forget those youthful emotions which fired our dreams and hastened our steps so long ago. The Scottish mountains, ice-clad and windlashed yet so accessible, then embodied all we desired in beauty and adventure.

I hope that this image still holds for every true mountaineer who looks to the northern hills in winter for the first time, whatever their age and whatever the level of their ambitions. And, should the story of our own adventures help in any way to awaken that vision, it will have proved its worth.

Martin Moran 1997

FOREWORD

Completing the Munros is a challenge. It was a challenge for the Rev A. E. Robertson who first achieved this goal in 1901; it was a challenge for the next Munroist, the Rev A. R. G. Burn in 1923, and it has been a challenge to many thousands since.

The list of Munroists, beginning with two reverend gentlemen, was itself a start to the long accumulation of statistics and records that have followed. The first lady, Mrs Hurst, entered the list in 1947 (also a husband-and-wife combination). There have been father-and-son records, people have gone solo, or in different seasons; Philip Tranter did them a second time and led to a row of multiple tallies. The ages of the oldest and youngest have changed steadily; even dogs have topped all the magic summits.

The game of Munro-bagging should have died with the maps going metric, which rendered obsolete the historic height of 3,000ft, but just enough people had completed the list, or were working on it, to ensure the game went merrily on. The number has multiplied since, and stood at 381 by the end of 1984*. It was natural enough to go off and do them all in a continuous 'walk' as I did in 1974. That jaunt has been repeated several times since. My mountain walk took 112 days of largely unspectacular and unhurried progress. Speed was far from my mind and I resented being given the 'fastest-ever' label. For this reason, if no other, I am grateful to Martin Moran's contribution to our crazy game. With his single winter's round, he, for his sins, became the fastest-ever Munroist! **

In some ways that too is incidental. It was the *winter* aspect which was the new challenge that Martin set off to tilt at – a real Don Quixote effort compared with my Sancho Panza one. Scottish winters can be fickle and, far from having endless snow which would have been a joy, Martin had to cope with every variety of nastiness except midges. I was lucky to join him for one day of glorious perfection on skis, but even that entailed cruel living in our frozen motor caravans. The winter

* The number of recorded Munroists had risen to 1,535 by the end of 1995.

** At the end of 1996 the record for the fastest completion was 51 days.

challenge is a mountaineering feat, not just a walking one, but then Martin is a lean, fit, well equipped Don Quixote. It only took 83 days! I think he gave his wife Joy who acted as support sufficient grounds for a divorce. It was a not unadventurous escapade.

I am delighted that their adventures have been set down. Our escapist's literature has been given a lively addition. Suddenly, after a decade with only *Hamish's Mountain Walk* for the armchair Munroist, there has been a flurry of books about the Munros. This one is different for here is a story of one man's accepted challenge. It gladdens my heart in these mean, grey days to see a young man putting feet to his rainbow dreams. Readers had best beware though: Munroitis is also a disease, a highly contagious one, which can be caught through the printed page. You have been warned.

Hamish M. Brown 1986

NOTE TO SECOND EDITION

There is little I wrote in 1986 that I would change. That the Munros are inspirational is seen in the growth in participant numbers, an indication of increased leisure opportunities and recognition of great enjoyment in this esoteric pastime. Martin's account has become a classic and I'm sure will inspire many in the years ahead to find and share the thrill of the Scottish hills.

Hamish M. Brown 1997

1
THE WINTER CHALLENGE

The Scottish Highlands have an aura that is unequalled anywhere within the small confines of the British Isles. Where else is there a natural domain of such infinite scale and unspoilt magnificence that one feels dwarfed and lost in its midst?

Think of any other upland tract – Dartmoor, Snowdonia, the Lakes: each one is touched and pressured, struggling for space, and even ravaged in places. The human hand is always in the view, and however lovely in certain parts or finer detail, Nature has surely lost her total freedom there in modern times. But up in the North you can still stand atop a lonely 'ben' and see no end or blemish to the expanse of mountain, loch and ocean that is spread out at your feet. The wilderness scene mocks our ego, and puts us in our proper place within the scheme of things, yet it also consoles and uplifts the spirit. And for the mountaineer, the array of peaks, which every Highland view includes, is an irresistible call to arms.

If the words ring true to those who trek and climb through the moist and misted months of Scotland's summer then they bear much stronger tone in the depths of the winter season. The numbers are fast growing of those who know the mountains to be at their finest when swathed in snow and battered by the year's worst storms, and no longer is one regarded as madly eccentric to take a winter climbing or skiing holiday in the Highlands.

The peaks may be relatively tiny in stature, but neither in shape, variety nor heart-stirring beauty do they yield much to any mountains in the world; and in winter their ferocious and unpredictable weather is renowned. They are a forcing ground of technique and experience, and generations of British mountaineers have cut their teeth on Scottish ice before progressing to the greater ranges. But it is unfair to treat the Highlands merely as a stepping-stone to bigger things: they have sufficient challenge of their own to meet the highest ambition.

This train of thought attracted me to the idea of a prolonged winter expedition in the Highlands which would explore their great potential for adventure; a single challenge involving every type of winter mountaineering skill from Nordic skiing to steep ice-climbing, and giving complete commitment to meet the hills in all their moods, both fair and foul.

The exploit would necessarily be contrived in its design and rules; yet without a code of ethics and a personalised objective is there *real* adventure left anywhere these days? The age of pure exploration is long past, and it is the style of achievement which now counts for all, whether it is yachting single-handed or climbing Everest without oxygen. To do it in Britain without expense and fuss would also help to prove the lie that modern adventure is the slave of commercial interests. But above all a trip was sought that would fulfil a longheld passion for the Highlands and, despite its trials and dangers, would be a thorough enjoyment to undertake.

And of course the solution was obvious – it had to be the Munros.

When Sir Hugh Munro, in 1891, surveyed and tabulated the Scottish mountains exceeding 3,000ft in height he would little have imagined that he was instigating a challenge and a tradition that ninety years later has achieved the status of a cult. What was probably for him a purely personal indulgence, is now a lifetime ambition for many thousands of keen hill-goers.

His original Tables gave 283 such separate peaks, a total now trimmed by resurvey and reappraisal to 277 in the latest 1984 edition. At the end of 1984, 381 climbers were known to have achieved the ascent of all, and there are countless others making determined progress towards their completion.

Notwithstanding the many fine summits below 3,000ft in elevation, and leaving aside the Hebridean islands, a Munroist can reasonably claim to have encompassed the greater length and breadth of the Highlands in his travels; so the apparently senseless mania of Munro-bagging does have a 'real' purpose which on its achievement ensures an intimate and extensive knowledge of the country. The lure of the unclimbed Munro takes the walker far beyond his usual haunts.

The 'Winter Munros' story properly begins in the summer of 1974 when Hamish Brown made the first non-stop traverse of them all in a continuous walk of 112 days. His feat is known to have been emulated twice, but of a winter grand-slam attempt nothing was heard. Understandably so, for whilst the traverse in summer is essentially a marathon walk with just a little rock-climbing on the Cuillin of Skye, in winter it is transformed to a mountaineering proposition of high order. And so, as one man's endeavour merely points out the things left undone, the winter gauntlet was thrown down, and I eagerly took it up.

Having set the objective some ground rules were required. First and foremost was the problem of timing. What, or to be more precise *when,* is 'winter' in the mountains? The tops can bear a complete snow cover in any month from October to May, yet in a lean year can be almost bare in the middle of January. If a deep coating of snow and ice was prerequisite to my every ascent, it could take several years to finish.

So the strict calendar season from 21 December to 20 March was selected as holding the greatest probability of winter conditions. This would follow the practice in the Alps where the calendar limits are applied rigidly to all claims of winter ascents. More excitingly, though, these limits thrust upon me a ninety-day target, which when divided into the 277 Munros determined a schedule that made my heartbeat race. Three summits per day – now that looked interesting! It would make a tough test of endurance at any time of year, but was it remotely possible through the dark days and snows of winter?

One thing was certain at the outset – the target was unattainable on a continuous journey, and would necessitate the major tactical concession of using motor transport between the peaks. Not only would this save the 500 miles of valley walking and cycling by which Hamish linked his mountains (imagine pedalling into a Force 10 gale on a late December night!) but would also give the crucial flexibility to choose whichever summits suited the prevailing conditions. The joy of continuity was sacrificed but the spice of adventure maintained, for even with motor support the scheme looked marginal.

Winter weather data for the Highlands make a fascinating study, but one which leaves the intending climber with few illusions about the challenge ahead.

The notion that the winter brings less rainfall than the other seasons is something of a myth. Records for both the west and east sides of the country show that the months from December to March take slightly more than their one-third share of the annual total, and of course much of the winter precipitation comes as snow. Nor in winter are the high tops any clearer of cloud. The nineteenth-century observatory readings for the summit of Ben Nevis gave a 75 per cent average frequency of hill fog between November and March.

Summit air temperatures, as would be expected, are depressed throughout the winter. On average, 6°C should be deducted from the sea-level readings to give the temperature at 3,000ft. On the summit of Cairn Gorm, 1,000ft higher, the *mean* air temperature in the four-month winter periods between 1979–82 was −3.4°C.

But it is winter winds that are most to be feared by the mountaineer. A compass will see you through the fog, and a good set of clothing can keep both the cold and snow at bay, but against the wind there is no answer. It slows the pace, saps the strength and sucks away the body heat – a triple threat in a single foe. Not only are natural windspeeds 50 per cent higher at 3,000ft than at sea level, but also the mountain topography has a compressing and channelling effect which markedly accelerates the flow. Just how many gales might be faced on the tops in those ninety days? The question was crucial to the whole venture.

The data for Cairn Gorm summit for 1980–1 gave an expectancy of 53 days with gales (ie, winds above 40mph) out of the winter's 90. The figure looked intolerable, and a more kindly interpretation was anxiously sought. After all, a day *with* a gale doesn't mean twenty-four hours non-stop, or in itself make all progress impossible. By making reasonable modifications the conclusion emerged that 32 days could be expected where progress was severely impeded (ie, winds between 40 and 60mph) and 10 where a climber would be stormbound (ie, greater than 60mph).

So those 277 peaks would have to be climbed in 80 days rather than 90, of which only 48 might allow full-scale expeditions. At least the storms would give some periods of rest!

October 1980: Sheffield
Having handed in my notice and abandoned an accountancy career a week previously, the preparations for the winter attempt had passed the point of no return. Even my wife, Joy, had with difficulty resigned herself to spending three months down here alone, keeping up her job and maintaining some semblance of security in our lives. And two months of hard running on our local hills and moors had built an enviable stamina and resilience to carry me through the coming struggles.

As usual the final light of a gloomy autumn evening saw me out training, pounding up a wooded clough towards the gritstone edges. With a lung-bursting effort I clambered to its top and turned to view the twinkling city lights behind. All was going well – the Munros dream was taking shape, its start just six weeks away. But at the beginning of the descent, without warning a shooting pain locked my knee-joint solid. Something was radically wrong. I tried to ignore it and went on, but ten more paces brought me staggering to a halt. It was four miles to limp back home, a slow and bitter walk.

Five days later I sat on the specialist's couch, and my worst expectations were realised as he delivered his solemn judgement:

'There's a piece of bone broken off your kneecap. If it isn't removed you will damage the joint, so you'll have to give up whatever it is you're planning to do...'

The anguish I felt when leaving that consulting room will forever haunt my memory. There I was, my spirit crushed, feeling an abject failure, out of work and without a future; so many people – companions, supporters and a local charity for whom I hoped to raise funds – to disappoint, and then facing the ignominy of asking for my job back. To my great gratitude I was re-engaged and the planned day of departure saw me back at a desk, pushing a pencil over ledger sheets once more, my escape hatch to the mountains firmly shut, perhaps for ever.

Yet this dream and challenge, so intently nurtured and pursued, was not to be forgotten. The knee recovered its strength from the operation. I worked and saved hard, climbed continuously and travelled afar. Self-confidence was slowly restored, experience broadened and four years later life was sufficiently organised to try a second time.

October 1984

Joy had noticed me creeping off upstairs of an evening for the last few months, and in her curiosity would come up to find me poring over Scottish maps, and scribbling notes of routes, distances and heights. She knew the truth without a word being spoken. The Munros game was on again!

But when the subject was broached and discussed, we made a firm pact to do it together. The lonely solo attempt planned in 1980 was perhaps ill-considered and very likely would have failed through lack of dependable help; for if there was one trump-card to play against the odds of wind and storm, then it was to have Joy with me, as companion, pacer, driver and provisioner. Most crucially, though, we would have each other for constant emotional support throughout the stresses of the journey. It would be an interesting test of marital harmony.

Joy was by no means overawed by the prospect. Her pedigree as a cycle tourer and marathon walker was considerable. Together we had walked the Pennine Way in winter, trekked over the deserted Norwegian plateaux in autumn, and now had just returned from an expedition in the Indian Himalayas. In fact she was so taken by the idea that she had already arranged the sale of our beloved terraced home even before my final decision to go was made. This was wisely deferred to the latest date possible for I wished no repeat of the cruel rebuff of 1980. First the strength of my creaking knee-joints needed to be proved conclusively, and so they were subjected to a summer's mountain guiding in the Alps, followed by four weeks under huge loads on a Garwhal glacier, before a public commitment was chanced.

This left us just six short weeks from design to launch. Transport and accommodation en route were our prime concerns, and were together solved by thumbing through the 'yellow pages' to the Motor Caravan Hire section.

'We don't usually get a lot of winter rentals. Will you be taking it far?' queried the owner of a white coach-built Ford transit which stood washed and polished in his drive.

'No, no, just up to Scotland to do a bit of hill-walking.'

'Oh well, that's all right then, but did I hear you right – it is three and a half months you want it...?'

We left him doubtful of our sanity but glad of the business all the same. The van was nearly new, fully insulated and with every imaginable fitment. All our hopes resided in its efficiency and reliability.

The trip was costed at £2,500, a figure which could be at least doubled if three months' loss of earnings was taken into account. And yet, retaining the style of simplicity and independence in which the venture was conceived, we sought no financial assistance from commercial sponsors. Berghaus served us proudly with their enthusiastic provision of boots, clothing and rucksacs of the highest quality. Their gear would never have a better testing. But that apart, we bore our own expenses.

However, we saw the expedition as an excellent vehicle to publicise and also sponsor a worthwhile charity. Two visits to the Himalayas had opened my eyes to the hopeless poverty and the environmental destruction with which India and many Third World countries are beset. The work of Intermediate Technology in providing new tools and methods to help regenerate and improve rural societies in these countries was already known to us through the incredible 2,000-mile run, over the foothills and passes of the Himalayas, which the Crane brothers had undertaken on its behalf in 1983.

We liked IT's preventive approach to famine. The adage comes to mind: 'If you *give* a man a fish you'll feed him for a day; if you teach him *how* to fish you'll feed him for life.'

It sounded perfect common sense, but would they risk taking on another crazy exploit to promote their cause? We wrote in hope, and were quickly accepted. Within a month the 'Summits for Survival' appeal was mounted, and a flourish of publicity arranged for our departure on 21 December.

But before enthusiasm ran away with reason, the results of those months of route-planning had to be assessed.

The required total of eighty day routes was drafted, giving the most efficient means of ascending every group of Munros. They varied from short return trips to climb the many isolated summits like Schiehallion and Ben Lomond, to extended traverses of the great multi-peaked ridges such as the Fannichs or the Mamores, and 25-mile Nordic ski-tours in the Grampians. To cover the remote areas such as Knoydart or Ben Alder Forest, around sixteen nights would have to be spent in camp, bivouac or, more likely, bothy shelters. The variety was intended. Each itinerary could hopefully be matched to the fluctuating weather – easy hills in stormy periods and the big traverses on clear days and moonlit nights.

The showpiece of the whole winter would be the Black Cuillin Ridge on the Isle of Skye, much the most difficult set of Munros in summer, and in winter conditions a major snow- and ice-climbing expedition, which has only been achieved in full by a handful of parties.

The allowance of ten rest or stormbound days could be extended by combining some of the shorter climbs, but only with difficulty given that the eighty planned routes themselves produced a taxing daily average of 1,675m (5,500ft) of ascent and 13 miles to cover all 277 summits.

Despite the van, our flexibility of movement was not unlimited and a logical progression had to be imposed to link the seventeen areas into which the Munro's Tables are divided. We chose to begin in the Southern Highlands where the better road network would give quick access to the peaks in the dark days of late December and early January. Then on into the central regions of Glencoe, Lochaber and Ben Alder; and as soon as the heavy snows arrived, we would take to skis on the rounded eastern hills. This would leave the final month from mid-February onwards to tackle the more difficult and remote peaks of the Western Highlands and the north, Skye included, where the two or three extra daylight hours could be of vital assistance.

The final details confirmed the initial inspiration. The Winter Munros looked at once a gruelling and rewarding challenge, and possessed the vital ingredient of uncertainty with which every adventure should commence.

2

THE STORM-TOSSED START

21–25 December:
Ben Lomond – Arrochar – Ben Lui –
Black Mount

The rain belted down onto Glasgow's streets, bouncing off the tarmac and sluicing into torrents along the gutters. The washed stone pavements gleamed brightly in reflection of the beams of passing vehicles as this urban flash-flood reached full flow. Overhead, twin lines of sturdy tenements formed a dark and glowering canopy to the drive along the Great Western Road. It was just the sort of night for seeking a warm fire and cheery company; yet we were bound far elsewhere, pitching ourselves into the wild blackness beyond the city limits.

Right turn at Anniesland Cross, a quick stop for petrol and then out towards Drymen. The neon threads of the city thinned, faltered and finally disappeared. Woodland and hedgerows now fringed the way; Balmaha's rows of buildings slipped silently past and the shores of Loch Lomond appeared on our left. Seven twisting miles further and we drew up at the empty parking lots by Rowardennan. In less than an hour of steady driving the transition was complete. We had entered the Highlands.

At last alone and unhitched from worldly cares, we were all but embarked on the reality of the voyage. But on top of excitement there was a tension induced by the elemental hostility of our welcome in the hills. Supper was sparse and brief, and my sleep was light. I suppose I tossed and turned in sympathy with the storm outside. Day one's diary recalled:

Heavy rainbursts drumming on the van roof, an incessant wind howling through the trees, and the crash of wavelets on the nearby loch shore all combined with my apprehension at starting to ensure a sleepless night.

At 7.35am in the dim light preceding dawn Joy and I began the climb to Ben Lomond. There were no fanfares, not even the click of a pressman's camera. Yesterday's brief fame on radio and television seemed far removed. Yet the absence of a public send-off was not in the least demoralising, for the expedition was envisaged from its inception as a solitary commitment, so this was the right way to begin.

The slopes of Lomond were washed and freshened by the overnight storm. Scattered residual showers drew moving curtains across the distant view, but they kept a respectful distance and we were spared a drenching. With new snow above half-height, a translucent mist clinging to the final ridge, and the summit artefacts bristling with ice hoar, the mountain bore a wintry hue, which seemed proper for the opening day of the season.

A touch of stage-fright was perhaps understandable on these momentous first steps. Had we pulled the rug from under our feet? For there we were, homeless, jobless and with a large hole in our savings account. But all lingering doubts and apprehensions were quickly suffused by a delicious sense of freedom as soon as the heights were gained. Such a euphoric feeling of release is always present on any excursion into the hills, however modest, but now, with an extended three-month sojourn stretching ahead, it was many times magnified. And of course there was a surge of relief just in reaching the starting line, for the bitterness of the failure in 1980 had by no means faded with time. Exactly a fortnight ago I had finished a last temporary stint of accountancy work, eight hours pinned down by computer prints and audit files, while Joy supervised the removal of our furniture into storage. Returning from work, suit and tie were cast aside, and we had squeezed into our new four-wheeled home – outcasts of our own choosing.

Emerging from the cloud on the descent we saw the rooftops of flats and factories in Dumbarton glistening in low-angled sunlight and throwing the wooded fringes and island studs of the lower loch into deep-textured contrast. Down there in the city people were pursuing the daily round, many working, others celebrating the coming Christmas break; but few able to envisage the magical world which we had entered only a few miles away. That sight confirmed the divorce from normality.

Sadly, the new-laid sheet of snow was unable to hide the unsightly scars of the track to the summit. This is one of Scotland's most frequently trodden paths, a proliferation of deep muddy ruts spreading into oozing swamps in all the hollows where countless pairs of feet have tried to skirt the slough, little realising that such avoiding manoeuvres merely fuel the galloping erosion process. The broad highway seemed a ridiculous over-provision for the needs of two lone winter wanderers. Ben Lomond, as the most southerly Munro, is certainly the most vulnerable to the unintended impact of mass usage, and it echoes the widespread human erosion which threatens to despoil the English Lake District. That our most popular hills are simply being 'loved to death' is beyond question.

The urgently needed restoration and long-term preservation of both the Ben and the delightful environs of Loch Lomondside are happily two of the central objects of an integrated tourist development plan currently being formulated for the area. The result may be a managed landscape that is distasteful to lovers of untrammelled wilderness. Yet without forceful conservation measures our scenic inheritance could become a degraded wasteland, no longer capable of inspiring the elation with which we were imbued on this first morning.

But however pleasing and uplifting was the ascent of Lomond, the knowledge that a second mountain lay on day one's menu did not escape my note, nor Joy's:

> *Chatting away about this and that, the descent passed easily, another happy outing together on the hills so it seemed – at least until we reached the van and I realised that our efforts today were far from over. No chance to rest, but a long tortuous drive to Glen Fyne ahead. Already the air had turned warmer and it was beginning to rain...*

Beinn Bhuidhe's rugged crest rises to 948m above the head of Loch Fyne, another isolated Munro, comfortably overtopping neighbouring hills and an obvious peak to combine with Lomond to complete a respectable day's work. Though Beinn Bhuidhe is only 20 miles further from Glasgow the ratio of visitors between the two must be in excess of a hundred times in the latter's favour. The imbalance is wholly unjust, for whilst Ben Lomond displays the greater poise and elegance of position, its rejected competitor is a real rough diamond and perhaps the more worthy mountain.

It transformed the airy sublimity of the morning into a gutsy struggle that bore a closer affinity with our long-term expectations. From the lower glen the subsidiary ridge of Beinn Chas had first to be crossed, itself a tough climb in long grass and heather clumps. Beyond lies 2 miles of indecisive knoll and hollow terrain before the craggy upper ramparts of the mountain are reached.

Though 1.30pm was too late to be starting it was the best we could manage, having driven the 40 miles from Rowardennan without delay and lunched en route. The rain was now entrenched for the afternoon. We dug our heels in too, but up on the snow-covered plateau were helpless to defy a tide of fatigue. Our legs lagged far behind the unyielding momentum of my watch, and the repeated rescheduling of our progress indicated an unplanned benightment on the summit.

In a gloomy dusk we tackled the final rocky slopes, bearing direct for the highest point up into dense cloud. I kicked steps in the deep slush and coaxed Joy upwards with genuine concern, for the exposure was sufficient to signal danger. As we emerged on top at 4.10, a strong sou'wester blowing volleys of soft hail pellets knocked us into a state of total disorientation. For a minute we groped about unsteadily until the crowning trigonometrical column was spotted. A foul night was gathering up here, no place for man or beast, and we promptly turned tail hoping to slither as far as possible down the mountain before total darkness forced a switch to torchbeams.

We carved a direct descent to Inverchorachan in the upper glen, happy to tramp the 2 miles of road back to our van at Merk Cottage so long as the hill was escaped quickly. But short cuts rarely give a smooth passage, and so it was that the map's gentle burn enlivened into a deep gorge when met on the ground. The 1:50000 First Series map for the area is merely a metric reprint of the old one-inch sheet, and lacks the precise detail of the new Second Series survey, which was due for completion in 1990. Confusion and bewilderment over the plethora of map scales and contour intervals used in the current Ordnance Survey lists were to beset my route-finding throughout the winter.

So with a frustrating reclimb and detour, and a forty-minute road bash, our first day was done – two Munros, 17 miles and 1,965m (6,450ft) of climbing. It had left the protagonists of the drama sore-footed, leaden-limbed and profoundly downhearted. The future looked appalling – a ninety-day treadmill due for summary resumption at the stroke of 6am tomorrow. My appetite for the 'delicious freedom' of the venture had somehow vanished, and the 'euphoric release' which I was applauding but a few hours previously now hung round my neck like a Derbyshire millstone!

A long sound sleep proved the best medication for these arid thoughts, compensating for my restless night at the foot of Ben Lomond, rekindling a weary body and revitalising the digestion, as was self-evident at a hearty 7am breakfast. Stewed prunes, muesli and two rounds of toast and honey: this morning menu was to become an unvarying ritual throughout the trip, but one that never palled in the slightest.

We were nestled in the bottom of Glen Croe, a snaking corridor linking Lochs Long and Fyne, and carrying the A83 on its interminable and thankless journey in search of Campbeltown down in the Kintyre peninsula. The glen lies in the midst of the jumbled hills of Arrochar, a cluster of rocky knuckles which provides Glasgow's closest high-level climbing grounds. These Arrochar 'Alps', as they are affectionately called, contain four Munros. Up until 1974 the total was five but Beinn an Lochain, standing above Rest and be Thankful at the head of the Croe, has suffered an ignominious demotion, a startling 20m being lopped off its altitude between successive editions of the Tables, the result of resurveying rather than subsidence. Now it stands as a proud 'Corbett' at 901m.

It is unfortunate that the district's most striking summit – the crooked beak of The Cobbler – also fails to surface from the 3,000ft waterline, but I was still left with a fine foursome, all of them Bens: Narnain, Ime, Vane and Vorlich. They give a big climbing day with 2,250m (7,400ft) crammed into a 12-mile itinerary. A pity then about the weather forecast – a deep depression in the Atlantic and a warm front tracking in from the south-west.

We climbed up the Croe Burn onto Bealach a' Mhaim, an unusual three-sided col. Such a configuration is notoriously confusing in mist, and sure enough we were 50m up on The Cobbler before I checked the compass for Narnain! Joy stayed with me for the first pair, then dropped down from Ime to take the van around to Inveruglas by Loch Lomond where my finish was planned, an arrangement that was often repeated in the coming months – risky maybe, but because of our utter interdependence we tended to feel closer when working apart than together.

As I pushed on through the fog and drizzle over the shaggy summit of Ben Vane, the windspeeds remained modest and the air warm.

continued to the 'plum pudding' dome of Meall nan Eun. Beyond lay the twisting barricade of Stob Ghabhar and the northern chain – so this unassuming top wrapped up the Black Mount Munros.

The day's five peaks had pushed us up 2,450m (8,000ft) of ascent yet it was now only 2.45pm, and there was plenty of daylight for a leisured amble down the Allt Ceitlein during which my eyes made a more detailed assay of Albannaich's cliffs and ravines. They unfolded sufficient winter climbing potential to amply repay a future visit.

As we turned into the main glen the day's tranquillity was abruptly shattered by the drone of a helicopter. Sure enough its winking light could be spotted hovering just above Starav's summit. The idea of the Glencoe rescue team doing a training exercise on New Year's Day was quite preposterous, so this must be a real accident. The helicopter made several sorties, then dropped and landed by the head of the loch, no doubt to unload the victim. No more than a minute later an ambulance pursued by a stream of cars roared past us on the road, creating the nearest to a traffic jam we had seen since leaving Glasgow. We later learnt that the climber had broken his ankle in a fall on the bouldery final slopes. His rescue had arrived at an opportune moment for the sunset glow was fast fading from the western sky as he was picked up.

Stretching out and sipping tea, it was now the time for a progress appraisal. A change of direction was needed, for our piecemeal campaign had completed the Etive, Orchy and Crianlarich hills – a total of 42 Munros just twelve days into the expedition. Already I had notched up 22,860m (75,000ft) of climbing and walked 150 miles, and if fitness was not exactly burgeoning forth, then the aches and strains most certainly were! Our plan was now to go back south to cover the rolling tops of Breadalbane, a three-hour drive to Glen Lyon before we could rest our weary heads. Only with sadness did we leave the lovely Etive, already thinking with regret of those roads and glens of Argyll that our journey would not traverse again.

4

THE SOUTHERN SWEEP

2–7 January:
Carn Marig – Ben Lawers – Glens Lyon and Lochay –
Schiehallion – Ben Vorlich

If a long drive in the black of night to an unfamiliar destination is tortuous, trying and even unnerving, then it pays fair compensation when one wakes at dawn to a new enticing world which is unveiled with a swish of the curtain. We had parked incognito on the roadside at Invervar, a hamlet in the middle reaches of Glen Lyon, barely able to decipher the treetops in the murky darkness of our arrival. So with eager eyes the bright scene of morning was absorbed.

Immediately a sylvan beauty was sensed in the tree-clothed strath that is lacking in the unkempt roughs of the western glens we had just departed. Neat copses in squares and strips sheltered solid, well kept farms and manses. Oceans of dead bracken spread up onto the higher grazings, and of wild mountain summits little could be seen. The impression was of a 'parkland', created and preserved by Man in his more tender guise.

We were reminded of The Cheviots, the local hills of our youth. Indeed, the topography hereabouts links this district more closely to the rolling Border counties than the rugged Highlands. A conglomeration of mica-schists, granulites, schistose grits and countless other metamorphosed bands form the hills, which are quite considerable in both girth and height. But forgetting the geological jargon and its infinite shades of classification, all these rocks have the common property that they wear well with age, stoutly resisting the march of time, and slowly rounding off into broad swells and pleasing convexity. They show few wrinkles or ragged edges, and have even survived the ravages of the Ice Ages with barely a scratch.

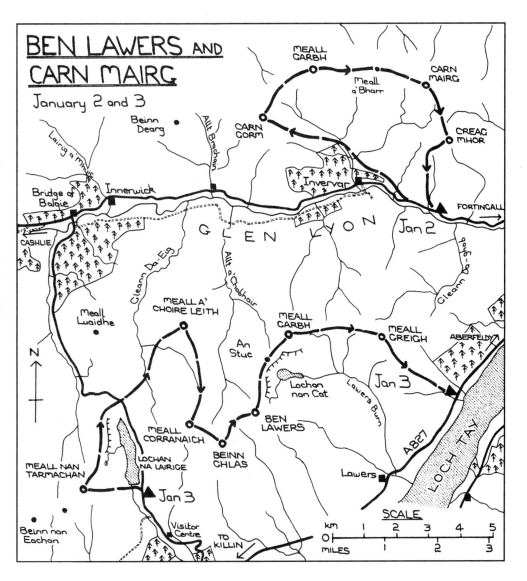

The Carn Mairg group – our first itinerary in the area – exemplified the scenery, four Munros and a handful of 'tops' all around the 1,000m mark, criss-crossed by sheepwalks and derelict fenceposts. They were a fast, simple round on this frost-hardened morning, and a welcome break after the rigours of Etive. The wind had slackened to an endurable tempo, and here lay a dusting of new snow which was absent further west. The Tilt and Shee hills to our north were also freshly whitened, bearing the delicate brushmark of passing cloudbanks which breezed in from the North Sea.

My first ailment of the trip was manifested today by the penetrating cold; not frostbite, nor even frostnip, but a distressing case of chilblains, a condition usually symptomatic of old age and a weak heart, and hardly flattering to an ardent mountaineer supposedly engaged in a heroic exploit. But lanky individuals like myself tend to have poor blood circulation and are therefore prone to such afflictions. Like frostbite you feel nothing when the icy wind is doing its damage. The exquisite pain comes later. That afternoon, with the van radiator belting out a scorching heat, my hands responded by itching and tingling relentlessly for an hour, while purple blisters of chapped skin swelled and cracked. My feet remained unscathed. They were perhaps working too hard to ever think about complaining! But however carefully my fingers were protected with gloves or mittens, this session of mild torture was often repeated in forthcoming evenings.

At 6pm we met Simon Stewart, the first of several supporters who had been arranged to join us at various stages through the winter. Having settled comfortably into a hermit-like lifestyle the idea of company was quite unsettling, especially in this case as we had not met Simon before. His acquaintance was arranged solely on the recommendation that he was a dedicated hill-man, and in the knowledge that he was only seventeen years old. An infusion of youthful energy would do us both a power of good, but there was a worrying doubt whether his experience and stamina would be sufficiently developed to cope with prolonged winter exertion. His father passed him into our care at the Bridge of Lochay Hotel by Killin – a long-haired gangling character, his beanstalk build not dissimilar to my own.

Any doubts over Simon's mountaineering pedigree were dispelled as soon as the ice was broken. After laconically dispensing the initial formalities, he opened up into some extended monologues which centred on three topics only – mountains, climbing and especially Munros! It was hard to believe that he was just eleven summits away from finishing not only the separate Munros but also the 240 additional subsidiary 'Tops' and, for completeness, all the 'deleted' Tops which have been relegated from older volumes of the Tables.

'Just to make sure in case any are resurrected in future editions', was Simon's rationale for this unprecedented mania.

My estimation of him was rising so fast that it was me who was left feeling like the young upstart, weakly clinging to a pathetic tally of eighty Munros before this winter's effort. We drove up to Lochan na Lairige for the night, high in the folded flanks of the Lawers group; at once a team knitted by a mutual respect, and looking to a common objective – the remaining sixteen Munros of the Breadalbane district, for which a maximum of five days was allowed. Simon's already intimate knowledge of the area would help greatly, for coming from Dundee these are some of his nearest hills.

Tomorrow's traverse of the seven Ben Lawers summits would be an ambitious opening gambit to this plan. Fifteen miles and 2,250m (7,400ft) of climbing would see us over the highest ground in the Southern Highlands, which is just 5m short of 4,000ft at the Ben itself. Simon promised me a fine, open, high-level walk, with a few surprises along the way.

Coping with three in the van at 6am in the morning promised to be a battle against anarchy, but Simon was effectively stunned to inaction by the proffer of a cup of tea up in his narrow bunk over the driving cab. You could read his thoughts – such unwonted decadence was totally beyond his own hard experience in the hills. He slept fully clothed, without a sleeping bag, presumably in a despairing attempt to simulate the open bivouac he so desired. While he drank, Joy and I self-consciously packed away our pillows and feather-down quilt and got breakfast started.

To be out on the icy road at 7am was a tribute to our powers of communal forbearance. Meall nan Tarmachan was the quickest Munro yet, merely an hour's climb from the lochan dam. Tarmachan at 1,043m crowns the eastern end of a four-peaked ridge which, if followed in full, would provide good winter sport. Of the other three tops Beinn nan Eachan looks sufficiently substantial to deserve a full Munro rating, but unaccountably it was ignored by Sir Hugh and has not since been elevated. His classifications never pretended to be anything other than subjective in basis, and though spared an extra effort it was aesthetically displeasing only to touch the edge of such an attractive group. It seemed that the real kernel of their challenge was being avoided.

This want of fulfilment had already been sensed on the Buachaille Etive Mor where of its trident of tops only the northernmost bears the full Munro stamp. One can while away a few stormbound hours devising a list of suitable candidates ripe for promotion, but as the preface to the current Tables comments: 'if effect were to be given to all the changes proposed the Tables would no longer be "Munros"'. And there are many who are downright indignant that the guardians of the Tables should assume the divine right to make any alterations whatsoever, except on the grounds of resurvey.

However, the crux of our day lay across on the eastern side of the Lairige. Thither marched Simon and I, while Joy descended to the unenviable tasks of laundering and restocking. From the summit of the Lairige at 540m we made, in Simon's words, 'a blistering fifty-minute ascent' of Meall a'Choire Leith, the northerly outpost of the group. Any secret hopes I fostered of 'burning off' the youngster on this section were emphatically dashed. The lad raced like a whippet!

The snowfields of Meall Corranaich were tackled more sedately, and debouched onto a slender summit crest that is barely hinted by the map contours. Hereon we were treated to an exhilarating ridge walk, sufficiently narrow and icy to merit our strapping on crampons for the final link from Beinn Ghlas to Lawers.

What a pleasure at last to have good reason for the crampons. Save for that treacherous runnel on the Buachaille, mine had so far served only as a fearsome decoration to the rucksac. Modern mountaineering opinion in Scotland recognises their obligatory use as the crucial hallmark of a true winter ascent. This is a complete reversal of pre-war tradition when nailed boots and alpenstocks sufficed for the most vertiginous passage, and crampons of any sort were ethically taboo. In that era many crampon-clad English climbers hastily left Ben Nevis with their ears burning from the wrath of some outraged doyen of Scottish climbing interests. How times change. Nowadays we all gleefully stamp about in our twelve-pointed foot-fangs even on the nursery slopes. But on testing ground they do ensure speed and safety, both of which were demanded on the crossing of An Stuc, a remarkably craggy top which took us from Lawers to Meall Garbh, the next Munro on the round. The Stuc and its south-east bastions above Lochan nan Cat are one of the few examples of glacial impact in the area, and the corrie formed a magnificent retrospect from Meall Greigh, the seventh and last of the day.

An hour ahead of schedule at 3.30 we met Joy by Loch Tayside. Our final descent was regaled with a mosaic of lush late autumn colours which was perfectly reflected in an unbroken loch surface, a scene which I later noted:

> ... was impossible to grasp without long pause and meditation. I regret my impetuous haste earlier in the day, and now am disgruntled. In future I must never rush such perfect days.

No change was observed in Simon's demeanour that evening. The Munros repertoire flowed on unceasingly, except when his jaw dropped in silent disbelief as we took our daily bucket wash.

Above the Bavarian splendour of Meggernie Castle and its estate, Glen Lyon splits two ways into wilder upper reaches, each fork containing a barren, dammed loch. Three isolated and unsung Munros flank the upper glens, each involving a separate ascent from valley level and in no way the 'semi-rest day' by which Simon later classified the outings.

We started from Loch an Daimh on the northern fork with an unenthusiastic plod to Meall Buidhe – its unimaginative name, 'the yellow hillock', being often used to delineate the retiring moorland tracts of the Grampians. Its unresisted admittance of Land Rover tracks to within a few yards of the summit further persuaded me to a derogatory impression, but rather than demeaning the qualities of the hill I felt greater disgust at the abuse which such tracks are perpetrating on our gentler heights. This was not an isolated reflection, but was raised with depressing regularity during my subsequent wanderings.

Conditions were misty and humid yet quite still, New Year's winds having faded without trace. This weather was as perplexing as it was pleasing, for early January usually sees the worst of winter's fury unleashed in great winds and blizzards. Taking the experience of early 1984 as a model had prepared me for Armageddon. Then we had spent New Year at Ullapool, and I vividly remember watching a factory fishing ship sheltered at the head of Loch Broom, pivoting on its anchor in endless circles throughout a two-day hurricane. Tempestuous conditions persisted without abatement to an unprecedented climax in the blizzard of 21 January in which five lives were claimed on the Northern Cairngorms. Thanks to a polar anticyclone settling over northern Europe, 1985 was producing less a battle for life than a fight against boredom. Only weak fronts trailing up the North Sea threatened to produce a whisper of dissent and no change was forecast.

Stuchd an Lochain bounding the south side of Loch an Daimh raised the day's interest a timely notch for it sports a precipitous northern corrie containing another Lochan nan Cat, which Simon told me is to be included in his list of 'the 100 finest campsites in the Highlands'. Peering into this mist-filled bowl we could see little of its qualifying merits, yet the depths exuded a mystery and charm which is absent on Scotland's countless Meall Buidhes.

With the addition of Joy who had driven round to meet us in the main upper glen at Cashlie we embarked as a threesome towards Meall Ghaordie, the third peak of the day, which fills the middle skyline between Lyon and Lochay and posed us an unvarying slope of 740m. Despite good company and the brief highlights of Stuchd an Lochain I could not shrug off the tedium of the day. Dismal, unchallenging weather, and this untroubled pace; an extra commitment was needed to bring the hills to life:

> Breaking decisively clear of Simon and Joy to avoid any suggestion of a race, I extracted a maximum physical effort and attacked Ghaordie with intensity, pounding feet and heart at full tilt up its bouldery slopes. Quite suddenly the lethargy lifted, and my perceptions were electrified. The scene whirled round my momentary glances – frost-furred heather, ice-caked rocks, a fleeing ptarmigan and the leaden expanse of Loch Lyon away behind. Wild and free I moved with the spirit of the hills, alone and lost in the immensity of Nature's empty theatre.

There can never be an excuse for finding any of this great country boring. The failure is surely of our own making. The climber must respond physically or else seek a little more closely, and far from being short-changed by the mountains there are many times when we fail to do justice to them, and simply do not give enough of ourselves. Up in an hour, sitting warm and snug in the summit shelter, there was a deep pleasure in having created a valuable experience from the day. However, the others were somewhat perplexed by the sudden hurry, having suffered no comparable urge:

'What on earth got into you? Got a train to catch or something?' they laughed, and made me feel most self-conscious.

The next night's halt in Glen Lochay lay only a mile to our south yet we were bound by our transport to return down Creagan an-t Sluichd to Lyon. But, although tortuous, the daylight drive back to Bridge of Balgie and over the ice-smeared Lairige road enabled our fullest appreciation of one of Scotland's longest and most varied glens.

Our day in Glen Lochay aroused special excitement, for there was a chance of achieving the complete circuit of the upper glen, a scheme which was undreamt of in my original routeplans, and which if effected would save a full day on the ninety-day target. The prospect was rendered possible only by the still air and hard snow. Joy wrote:

We left in the dark at 7am, our spirits hungrily awaiting the clear dawn
views which would meet us on the tops; 9,000ft of ascent, five Munros and
21 miles awaited our steps.

The day's tops encompassed the 'Forest of Mamlorn', or King's Forest. It is hard to conceive that these hefty grassy bulwarks were clothed with trees within historical memory. No remnant can now be traced save on the vegetated cliffs where the odd withered rowan still ekes out a living, safe from the predations of sheep and deer.

Joy's prediction of summit views went sadly awry. First light found us lost in dense fog somewhere on the southern shank of Beinn Heasgarnich. Simon's canny route-finding took us to the highest point after many a bemusing undulation, but this mist already threatened to curtail our ambitions. Daylight's few hours would not accommodate complex navigation in addition to the exertions of the itinerary. Trooping down off the west ridge our hearts already were drooping in this knowledge, when as if by magic a great hole was torn in the vapours to reveal the white ramparts of Creag Mhor looking every inch an Alpine 'Nordwand' in its framed isolation.

The day was saved, and we hurried on, weaving a satisfying line up those shadowed icy slopes to pop out into blazing sunshine just 10m from the cairn.

Hereon a pattern was established, with myself striding a little ahead lost in introspection. This unceasing effort and especially the thought of the hours, days and months to come required my total concentration, numbing any conversational capacity. Happy chatter and laughter floated forwards in lilting waves, so my silence was more than compensated for by the remainder of the team.

Ben Challum, the figurehead of the upper glen, was the next and most crucial object of the day, but first the transverse top of Cam Chreag had to be crossed, our attempts to contour it falling foul of countless streams of water ice. Then from the pass at the head of Allt Challum came a cruel 400m climb to the top. We were all starting to tire but it was gained on time at 1pm. A tiny wooden cross adorns the cairn, a delicate gesture unique on Scotland's high summits, and a miniature imitation of innumerable such crucifixes and statuettes which mark the peaks throughout the Italian Alps. Especially here, in this far-flung outpost of European civilisation, its discovery provoked a moment of quiet contemplation.

A biting cold enforced a swift resumption, despite the glorious views which the unrolling mists had bequeathed. A 600m drop before gaining the southern side of the watershed called for a stiff mental resistance. How tempting to quit the challenge and slink back down into the glen! Down the chilly snowfields of Challum's north-east spur, across the ice-clogged burn, then up the green and sunbaked south-west flank of Meall Glas. It was 3pm, and ninety minutes of light were left. That last enticing summit, Sgiath Chuil, could just be attained by sunset.

The southern pair are the lowest of the round and lack the class of Challum or Creag Mhor, but they are marvellous viewing stations for the empty quarters of Mamlorn as well as affording majestic prospects of the Lawers assembly and the massive Crianlarich silhouettes. But hardly had Joy and Simon touched the cairn of Meall Glas than they were motioned to continue. How surly and taciturn they must have thought me. Yet there could be no relaxing until that fifth top. Joy's hind view of me possessed a healthy irreverence:

> On the descent of Meall Glas, Martin was seized in an extra flurry of energy, and bolted off ahead like a deer that has scented Man in its nostrils. We followed some way behind, appreciating the frozen ground; none of the peat bogs that I remembered from our previous visit.

Stopping on the bealach, with only 300m to go in the evening gloaming, Simon ambled up in the rear, laid down his sack and ingenuously declared: 'Look, I'll go down and take your loads. You'll be much faster, and anyway I can make a meal for when you return.'

We were momentarily left speechless in the face of this selfless offer; but steadfastly refused to accept. This great day was a team effort to be completed by all. But underlying our refusal there was surely a slight fear of the disastrous recipe Simon might concoct out of our pile of pulses, vegetables and spices, for he had exhibited absolutely no culinary skill during his stay other than for boiling mountainous bowls of porridge, whilst his only other dietary preference was for an endless stream of Mars Bars and fruit pastilles!

So with a full moon rising over Lawers, and a pink sunset fringing Ben Lui, we stood atop Sgiath Chuil – a very happy trio, but all on our last legs after much the hardest day of the trip so far. The round should be high on the list of objectives for the ambitious hill-walker. Endless peat groughs by the Lubchurran Burn laboured our final descent, and it was well after darkness when we wearily reached the valley road and tramped the last mile to the public roadend at Kenknock. At least we were assured of a delicious celebratory spaghetti expertly cooked under Joy's safe guidance.

The 1,083m cone of Schiehallion was now the only outstanding peak in the Breadalbane area. Its shapely pile has been one of the Scottish Tourist Board's greatest assets. With the foreground of Loch Tummel or Rannoch, here is all the romantic beauty of the Highlands captured in a single view, which though somewhat hackneyed nowadays is nevertheless an inspiring prospect. It is a mountain that people approach with the greatest of ardour yet rarely climb more than once, for its unrelieved scree and heather slopes have little intrinsic interest that would beckon a return visit.

The peak presented a relatively short interruption to a day of rest and recuperation, but the chance of a lie in bed was passed, our mental alarm clocks throwing us wide awake at the normal hour of 6am. At Killin it was lightly snowing. One of the North Sea fronts had breached the Highlands, and we were to be denied all impression of Schiehallion's famous symmetry by dense milky cloud.

By 11am we had roused sufficient energy to drive round by Fortingall to the Braes of Foss car park and commence the climb. Here was a typical example of Forestry Commission 'recreational management' – neat parking lots, waymarked nature trails, and the marching columns of pines – all very attractive in isolation, but tedious in its proliferation throughout the British uplands. The scenic diversity, so prized and vaunted as an unmatched quality of our small islands, could easily be reduced to a dreary monotone.

Above the trees a maze of peaty tracks desecrated the lower slopes. Without a lofty summit to behold, our eyes inevitably focused on this pointless spoilation. Man's lust to wander at his individual will often frustrates the most worthy attempts at environmental control. Schiehallion is clearly a very popular hill, and it is sad that its distant inspiration is not fulfilled on detailed acquaintance. The paths coalesced on the long east shoulder, where a strong gale bent us over like the newly-planted saplings in the woods below. The ascent seemed untowardly hard, for we all carried mental hangovers from our exertions in Mamlorn, and were pleased to have the job done inside three hours.

Driving down to Crieff in the afternoon we touched the edge of the richer rural garden of the Central Lowlands. The lush grazings, fattening livestock, deciduous copses, mown lawns and scattered golf links all struck an unsettling contrast to the snowy heights just quitted. This would be our last contact with lowland scenery for some time, but its lazy Sunday atmosphere was no attraction for us to stay.

Simon's time with us was now over, and his parents were already waiting in the town centre to collect him, bursting with pride and affection while Simon shrank in embarrassment. His dour persona is but a weak disguise to a boundless love of the mountains, a warmth of spirit and a lack of ego that is unusual in someone so young*. A couple of months later we read with pleasure but no surprise of his completion of the Munros and Tops – Blaven on Skye was his final peak. Two months before his eighteenth birthday he thus became the youngest Munroist to have completed the peaks without adult support, three months ahead of Andrew Nisbet who had been the existing holder of this juvenile crown since 1972**. His company had been an inspiration, as well as a sometimes painful mirror to our adult affectations. So, feeling just a little bereft, we turned the wheel back into the hills, to Glen Lednock above Comrie. Our Breadalbane plot had borne full fruit, and only three summits remained of the southern sweep.

There was an unholy row on Ben Chonzie at 8am the next morning – a din of bickering voices which even woke the sheep and sent them scurrying off into the dank mist.

'You're just an elitist; always preaching to people,' came Joy's yell from the rear.

'What's wrong with beliefs?' I roared back, and stalked onwards.

A minute later came the despairing female scream, 'Wait for me; if you don't stop, I'll...!'

Some faintly tendentious remark I had forwarded about the environmental dangers of new ski development had goaded Joy into stubborn defence, for she loves downhill skiing and views it as a wonderful family pastime. And as our tempers frayed we swopped a crescendo of insults, until I was reminded of Robert Louis Stevenson's perceptive

---

* Simon Stewart now pursues his career as a geophysicist with the same passion as he did the Munros, and remains an active hill-goer.

** Lynn Batty at eleven years is the all-time youngest, if Hamish Brown's dogs can be excluded from the count! However, her round, which was completed in 1995, was done under parental supervision.

observation that: 'to live out of doors with the woman a man loves is a fellowship more quiet even than solitude'.

Chonzie was but a passive spectator to this display of marital discord. The clouded tussocky climb up from Invergeldie held no great appeal, but the hill carries an aura of timeless peace, which should have been respected. It is the only Munro in the upland country between Loch Tay and Strathearn, a barren plateau of rough grazings, which is dissected by glens of great charm, and crossed by a series of old droving paths.

Our fracas quickly subsided once we were back within earshot of the farm, but it had given immediate relief. Freed from the confines of etiquette in Simon's company, we could blow some steam off the conflicting pressures and strains which each of us felt. Soon we were laughing again, and the contest was quickly forgotten under the urgencies of the moment, for I was due back at Comrie by 10am to give a live telephone interview for a Tyneside radio station. After more than a fortnight this was the first reminder that we were embarked on a public enterprise.

With only minutes to spare we found a vacant call-box…

'Tell us, Martin; what's it like up there in the frozen North?' asked the interviewer.

Looking out of the sun-glinted kiosk panes at the Monday morning scene in Comrie – delivery vans unloading, housewives shopping and old ladies gossiping – I could easily have shattered his vision of the snow-bound wastes, but cheekily chose to foster the deception.

'Pretty rough', I replied, as a ten-ton lorry rumbled by. 'We've got severe conditions here – fresh snow, a biting cold wind and deep frost!'

'Thank you and good luck, *Mr Munro!*' he concluded.

After that little farce it was a pleasure to get back to the tangible world and tackle the broad bulk of Ben Vorlich, starting from Ardvorlich on the south side of Loch Earn. With its craggy partner, Stuc a'Chroin, Vorlich is the first rugged mountain outline to arrest the eyes on the approach from Stirling to Callander, the pair forming a north-east continuation of the Trossachs country.

However, Joy was profoundly depressed by yet another 'heads down' climb:

> *Glen Vorlich was so beautiful that I wanted to tarry awhile and meditate on the splendour that the mountains offer. But no; each Munro seemed to be*

a target to be conquered in the fastest time possible. Martin's intensive mood is getting on top of me, but I guess he knows that his goal requires total concentration. It was a relief for me to turn back from Vorlich's summit whilst Martin made for Stuc a'Chroin. As the tenseness unwound on a leisurely descent, my animosity towards him disappeared and I felt my spirits uplifted; so it was a smiling Joy and a hot drink that greeted his return at 3pm.

By contrast I viewed the climb as:

… a great romp – hard, dry, direct and airy with the summit trig visible all the way – no false tops on Vorlich!

Stuc a'Chroin then provided an icy and intricate scramble through its north-eastern ramparts. Morning mists had cleared but valley fog still clothed the broad Forth valley. Only the rocky neck of Stirling pierced the blanket. And lo and behold, down to the south-west there were the razor-edges of Arran's peaks poking up in the gap of the Clyde. Central Scotland was mapped at my feet and resting easy under a docile mass of rippled cloud. With a neat contour under Vorlich and a heathery descent of Coire Buidhe I was soon trotting back to Ardvorlich. Sections One and Two of the Tables were now complete, and we could joyously turn a page and sense real progress.

5

INTO WILDER DOMAINS

8–13 January:
Glencoe – Glenfinnan – Ben Alder Forest

The Buachaille Etive Beag resembles an upturned clipper's keel, sandwiched between and truncated by the Lairig Eilde and Lairig Gartain – a mountain shunned by the majority in favour of Glencoe's more famous peaks. Yet transported to the English Lakes or Snowdonia, it would be idolised as an upthrust of unparalleled grandeur. Such are the quality and extent of the Highlands that even great peaks are often forgotten.

Lacking a convenient connecting ridge to any other summit, the Beag had to be tacked awkwardly onto the Bidean nam Bian to effect my morning's scheme of completing the southern side of the glen. The Aonach Eagach would follow after lunch. Vaulting ambition was galloping ahead of my good reason. Not content to have compressed my schedule by one full day in Glen Lochay, I now greedily aimed to devour another.

With cocksure enthusiasm I marched off at 6.40am into the moon-shadowed depths of Lairig Eilde, and immediately lost the track. Instinctive navigation struck a diagonal line up towards Stob Dubh, the mountain's southern and higher top, but my intuition served me ill. Ice-filled gullies tumbled down the flanks, barring progress and enforcing a series of slippery detours to gain the miniature coire that is cradled under the summit shoulder. Up here, the fines of the screes weirdly crunched and collapsed under my step. A perplexed examination revealed dense spillikins of ice needles raising the pebbles several inches into suspension – the remarkable result of prolonged frost expansion of the ground moisture.

As I hoisted myself onto the lofty summit perch an equally strange and macabre view met my gaze. Rising dawn dyed the boiling mass of westward cloud a lurid mauve. The Bidean formed a sheet-white shroud beneath, whilst a bright full moon above kept guard over this witch's brew of colour, which surely heralded a calamitous storm.

However, only a wet cloak of mist transpired, and it enveloped the climb to Bidean without a single breath of breeze. The spidery tentacles of Glencoe's crowning peak give some of Britain's best ridge-walking. The route over Stob Coire Sgreamhach passed the rocky prow of the Sron na Lairig – a first-rate winter scramble in itself – then encircled the clefted head-wall of the fabled Lost Valley before ending abruptly on Bidean's tiny top. But today the climb took the wind out of my sails:

> *Due back in the glen by 11am I was forced to hurry, but the sticky humidity slowly suffocated my energy and stifled the composed determination with which I had set out. I slumped down on the summit lathered in sweat, salopettes torn, and both toes of my gaiters unstuck and flopping uselessly off the boots.*

With a mask of overnight powder snow obscuring the iced track the descent served only to weaken my resolve. First, a narrow nape of rocks lured me off-route leftwards until I was teetering on the brink of the Diamond Buttress. Later, dropping off the north-east ridge into the Lost Valley, a hidden ice patch upended me with such violence that my head ricocheted perilously close to its brick-like surface. And finally, the mass of jumbled boulders which blocks the mouth of the valley triggered many a bone-jarring slither.

Half-an-hour late, wet and enfeebled I reached the van. Alan Thomson was already waiting. Alan is a freelance journalist, resident in Glencoe for ten years, a climber of considerable experience and a member of the local rescue squad. Naturally he was taking a close interest in my travels. His chirpy chatter over coffee cheered my spirits, but he professed a cautious scepticism about my chances of success.

'Things are going well for you now, Martin', he would say. 'But it's certain to come in the next two weeks. In last year's storms the rescue lads spent three days just digging cars out of the road in the glen, never mind tackling the mountains!'

Perhaps he saw a ripe potential looming for an epic melodrama with me as the missing victim and Joy as his 'femme fatale'!

The mist and drizzle precluded our planned photographic session on the Aonach Eagach that afternoon. Its postponement offered me the desired excuse to terminate the day. Bidean had effectively squashed all zest. We drove on to Fort William, and new intriguing mountain domains opened on all sides. But first the mundane task of laundering had to be attended to. Caol's 'washerama' must surely be Scotland's slowest, and delayed our exploits by nearly two hours, sufficient time to shrink my salopettes to an alarming tightness.

A fifteen-minute drive whisked us away from the looping streets, drab housing and smoking mill of Corpach and into a fiery mountain sunset at Kinlocheil, a transition of worlds that was barely comprehensible in its immediacy. We were treating ourselves to a brief preview of the West Highland challenges that were to be our succour in the months to come, although the three Munros to the north of Glenfinnan posed such an arduous tour that one would wonder whether we were seeking reward or penance. I would be glad of my afternoon's rest come tomorrow night.

Gulvain it seems is *not* Scotland's best-loved mountain. Even the Gaelic forefathers must have turned up their noses, for its likely derivation 'Gaor Bheinn' means 'hill of filth or faeces'. My district guide drily notes it as 'a somewhat uninteresting mountain', whilst Hamish Brown failed to offer a single word of flattery as his account of his 1974 walk passed this way. My friend Chris Dodd was more to the point. He climbed the hill on a six-day round of twenty-four of the Section 10 Munros in 1983 and libelled it thus: 'The slopes are endless; definitely the most depressing mountain in this area.'

Yet no hill should be damned before being sampled, and we paid it eager court, for here and northwards to Glen Shiel lay a grandiose mountain realm, which we were penetrating for our first time.

Black ice flowed in streams of treacle down the track from Wauchan, making the night approach up Gleann Fionnlighe a trial of patience and nerves. Passing the farm buildings gave us a second waking, as if the 5.30 alarm hadn't been enough:

> Glancing beyond my torchbeam I was suddenly confronted by a ghoulish white wraith, its two eyes gleaming like gemstones. I started back in panic, fully convinced that I was encountering some sort of spectre. Only when I dared a second look did I discern a docile farm horse trotting away.

The dawn which found us toiling up Gulvain's south ridge came as a greater relief than usual after this apparition. Frigid still air, the bone-like ground and a distant haze today gave the mountains an especially empty and soul-less tinge, to which the twin-topped summit ridge formed an airy viewing platform.

Endless waves of jagged ridges stretched to our north, frozen like skeletons in a prehistoric museum. Most prominent was the long Glen Garry spine which could be traced westward from Gairich over its contorted vertebrae to the culminating horn of Sgurr na Ciche. In a one-day traverse this was schemed as my route of entry to the Knoydart peaks beyond, but now, beholding the prospect in its awesome reality, my paper plans promptly crumpled.

After an icy descent hot coffee and sandwiches were well in order to console our spirits. Our route now manoeuvred a northern circuit of the two Streaps which could aptly be renamed 'the steeps' for they are undoubtedly the finest hills in the locality and sadly miss the Munro mark by only 5m. In recompense for their avoidance we faced a tough watershed crossing from Gleann Camgharaidh to Gleann a'Chaorainn, both deeply incised valleys twisting tortuously towards Loch Arkaig. In this outback we were forcibly reminded of the increased commitment of winter travel west of the Great Glen. The security of the Mallaig road here lay fully 8 miles through an untracked pass to our south.

Mounting the crest of Sgurr Thuilm brought the return of reassuring views – the Glenfinnan rail viaduct and the Jacobite monument standing guard to the head of Loch Shiel. Without further detour we could hold the main ridge to our third Munro, Sgurr nan Coireachan, but quite suddenly the going became rugged and broken, rock slabs and dykes outcropping at awkward transverse angles to slow the pace by half – another foretaste of the 'rough bounds' of Knoydart.

The long wedge of Loch Morar stretching out to the sun-dappled sands of Arisaig afforded a majestic view from Coireachan's top. The loch plunges to a maximum depth of 310m, yet is barred access to the sea by a slender neck of solid land at its outlet. What gouging processes could have formed such a trench? At least a 1,300m thickness of over-lying ice was estimated at the height of glaciation; but why the overdeepening at this particular point? Even the expert glaciologists are still hard pressed to produce a convincing account of fjord origin.

We quickly turned our steps down the side of Sgurr a'Choire Riabhaich as another cold night gathered; but, as is my wont, I would several times pause to peek down slanting gully shafts. How deep, how steep; the lure of the unknown mapping my future life! At the price of a few miles walk-in there is a wealth of winter pioneering still awaited in these hidden corries; nothing on the scale of Nevis, granted, but huge scope for private and more personal experience far from the 'madding' crowds.

A perfectly drained and graded stalker's path cushioned the final drop to the valley at Corryhully, yet was obviously disused. We soon encountered the reason – a brand new forestry road carving a swathing scar into the heart of the hills. Shocked? Oh yes. Outraged? Without doubt... yet we still used it to speed our final miles.

The main road was black and deserted. A long wait or a longer walk back to Kinlocheil? We were obliged to wait under the firm orders of our buckling legs. Ten silent minutes ensued, and then a lonely shaft of light broke the western darkness. As the engine droned closer our hearts raced in hope. The blinding beams swung round the last bend. We had brief seconds to make our case, and some grovelling tactics were employed. With theatrical bows and expansive sweeps of our outstretched arms the lorry was implored to an immediate halt.

In magnification of our 20-mile trek the driver was completing a 200-mile nightmare of ice-bound single tracks, his weekly delivery run round the scattered hamlets of Moidart, Sunart and Morven. These little-known mountain tracts to our south form the largest area in the Highlands without a Munro, yet possess sixteen separate peaks above 2,500ft, a rich harvest for the 'Corbett' collector. We tumbled out and back into our van a little after 6pm. Fresh clothes, a wash and a hurried meal and we were driving again, down through Spean Bridge onto the Loch Laggan road. Tomorrow was almost upon us before we could catch a breath of reflection on the events of today. Only the dull throb of fatigue in our legs left a lingering memory of the Glenfinnan heights. And old Gulvain? Well, it's not such a bad mountain after all.

Fersit, 8am – a string of silent cottages spanning the River Treig. It is deep in the raw middle of January; seventy Munros are climbed but a hell of a lot more remain to do, and a colourless dawn reveals the many dim shapes of untrodden peaks. Inside our cocoon of warmth I am slumped forward, arms propped against the breakfast table, bloated, befuddled and hungover. A second potato scone dripping with margarine is unwillingly forced down with a swill of tea. Eight hours of sleep has done little more than scratch the eyelids, and a well of fatigue remains untapped.

Four days' supplies are now to be packed and then shouldered for our first extended bothy trip of the winter through the Ben Alder Forest, the heart of the Central Highlands. Trust the weather and take our chance, though it could so easily snow today. Excited anticipation is absent. Only an instinctive dread preys on my soul that exhaustion is lurking just round the corner. After three weeks of preliminary sparring the pace has stepped up. My real Munros battle is started at last:

> We noticed a covering of fresh snow which yesterday's western hills had escaped and which was thick enough at lower levels to reveal countless imprints of the overnight couches of red deer. The 30lb loads spared us no effort breaking trail onto Stob Coire Sgriodain, and our 10^1/$_2$-mile route to Loch Ossian quite innocently took on an epic quality.

The day's three Munros – Sgriodain, Chno Dearg and Beinn na Lap – form the turning point of 'Ramsay's Round', one of the most taxing mountain tours in the Highlands. Extending a one-day circuit of Glen Nevis originally devised by Philip Tranter in 1964, Charlie Ramsay's jaunt takes in not only the Mamores and Ben Nevis–Grey Corries ridges, but adds the Loch Treig group of hills to give a total of 24 Munros, 58 miles and 8,530m (28,000ft) of ascent. The attempt was made over 8–9 July 1978. Charlie crossed these Loch Treig hills in the black of night and then made some appalling route-finding errors in mist on the Grey Corries, before flying down Ben Nevis in 30 minutes to arrive at the Youth Hostel starting point just 2 minutes inside the target time of 24 hours. There have been few takers for repeats even among that rare and crazy breed of fell-runners, and Charlie's record still stands. This is the greatest number of Munros that has ever been climbed in a continuous one-day effort.

Knowledge of such a magnificent achievement severely dented our pride as we struggled to complete even the easiest quarter of the round:

> We shared the lead over Chno Dearg, then ploughed down into the deep defile of Allt Feith Thuill which isolates Beinn na Lap and presented a major potential impasse. A bar of fudge was requisitioned from tomorrow's rations and divided two ways to avail the 400m climb to the last summit. Slowly and stoically we made the long haul. Had there been a wind to disturb this sullen afternoon it would have bowled us over and back down, so weak did we feel. The sight of Loch Ossian's wooded shores

km 0 1 2 3 4 5

miles 0 1 2 3

SCALE

BEN ALDER FOREST

January 10–12

was gratefully received from the summit tumulus, our focus immediately homing onto the tiny Youth Hostel building perched on a headland on the opposite bank, for there lay our promised sanctuary for the night.

One hour later at 4.30pm we were 'knocking' at the front door. The hostel is staffed only during the summer months but we had been assured by the Scottish YHA that it is left unlocked in the winter. Rattling and wrenching at the handle brought not an inch of response:

I was already reviewing the habitability of the surrounding woodstores and hutches, and composing an enraged letter to the authorities when a soft grinding and a delighted shout came from the rear. Joy had found an entry, and we could escape the repellent gloom without for a wood-panelled interior.

Then to compound our woes the stove refused to work at more than a pitiful hiss. Cartridge and burner were of different makes and refused to marry. Mid-way through our protracted cooking operations another couple arrived, kindled a roaring wood fire in minutes, then nipped out for a dip in the loch. What vigour and energy! Where on earth was ours? After stealing a seat by their fire for an hour, and plundering some leftover food from the kitchen we slunk off to bed, profoundly concerned how we would cope with Ben Alder itself tomorrow. That cold was getting right to our bones.

Strath Ossian with its loch, lodges, plantings and railway halt is a happy oasis of shelter in a cirque of bare hills. To leave its harbour in the black of night was not easy, especially in the grim recollection of the tragedy of 1951. Five climbers were overtaken by a snowstorm as they attempted to reach Ben Alder Cottage by Loch Ericht from an overnight bivouac at Ossian, almost on the exact line of today's planned route. One by one, four of them yielded to exposure. The fifth member of the party, a girl, survived.

   As we traversed Carn Dearg and Sgor Gaibhre, the two Munros to the south of the loch, any dismal thoughts were dispelled by a sudden clearance of the sky. A light east breeze rolled back the blanket of leaden clouds and a golden dawn flooded the horizons. Blizzards forgotten, this was going to be a marvellous day:

> Immediately my senses perked up, and abandoned reserves of strength returned unannounced. Purgatory changed to enlightenment as an audacious change of plan emerged. Today's route was originally conceived to continue direct over Ben Alder to Culra Bothy, leaving the Aonach Beag group to the north of the Bealach Dubh for another full day. Now, if from Sgor Gaibhre I crossed the Uisge Labhair and took in the three main Munros on Aonach Beag I could then return across the bealach to capture Alder tonight and make a whole day's saving – a scheme so obvious, yet never considered until that flaming orb rose in the east. Who says that we aren't all sun-worshippers at heart?

Only with Joy's assistance could this possibility be realised. Having dropped the 450m to Uisge Labhair we rearranged the loads, and as I departed for Beinn Eibhinn burdened by little more than a camera and waterproofs, Joy tottered off towards the Bealach Dubh, and thence the bothy, dwarfed by a lop-sided sack crammed to overflowing with our overnight kits. No wonder she failed to share my sudden inspiration:

The snow was deep and powdery and within a mile the track petered out leaving me to settle my own route to the top of the pass. The load was doubly cumbersome on the boulder-strewn climb and I resorted to counting my steps to keep up any momentum. I occasionally looked up to see Martin strolling across his next Munro, having a great time no doubt! However my own thoughts centred on reaching the welcome of the bothy... a hot cup of tea and a fire...

The Bealach Dubh is an important natural thoroughfare linking the Spey Valley to Ossian and then Glen Nevis, and cuts an impressive slice through the centre of the Alder plateau. Surprising then that it has no well defined walker's path. Stalking tracks abound but none traverses the bealach, for here is a boundary between estates and the tracks of each pursue independent courses up into their respective deer retreats.

The 30-mile trek from Dalwhinnie through to Glen Nevis is one of the Highlands' grandest, crosses no public road, yet is well supplied with bothy shelters en route. It forms the central section of the 'Scottish 4,000ft Munros' tour, often being done during the night to link the daytime ascents of the four main Cairngorms and the Lochaber quartet.

Once reached, the Aonach Beag peaks gave a narrow and exhilarating ridge-walk, their summit snows burnished to a hard windcrust in contrast to the valley powder. Beinn Eibhinn's English appellation, 'the delightful hill', was no misnomer on this sparkling day. After crossing Joy's staggering line of prints on the bealach a dogged effort took me onto Alder's broad summit where one encounters a perfect piece of Cairngorm-style plateau terrain.

Ben Alder attained, the day was won, leaving me the sunset hour to wander wearily over Beinn Bheoil stopping frequently with the excuse of making identity checks on the surrounding ranges. The sight of the Breadalbane massifs across the southern end of Ericht jogged my memory to the happy days so recently spent there, whilst the nearby view across the parallel spurs of Alder, Aonach Beag and Beinn a'Chlachair was quite perplexing in its longitudinal regularity.

Even from the top of Bheoil's northern spur a welcoming light was espied in the bothy window, hastening me towards its comfort. Joy had suffered similar delusions a few hours previously:

Culra at last appeared – but there was no sign of life; no smoke from the chimney. I crept into its dark and musty inside cell. There was no fresh stack of dry branches and peats, only a few green lumps of soaking

bogwood. Oh well, I thought, I may as well have that cup of tea. I grasped
the blackened kettle to fetch some water only to scream at the sight of a
drowned mouse floating inside. Utterly dejected I settled into my sleeping
bag for a long wait…

Just before 6pm I plunged across the burn and cheerily hailed at the
bothy door. To my dismay a scene of Dickensian misery met my gaze
within. Rivulets of damp streamed down the walls, a pile of rotten wet
wood was belching smoke in the fireplace and huddled beside a single
flickering candle was Joy, wrapped in her sleeping bag, only a pallid
face and weary eyes poking out, and trying to coax a flame from that
damned stove of ours. She looked for all the world like Little Dorrit
sitting at her sewing in Bleeding Hearts Yard. Culra *is not* one of
Scotland's most luxurious mountain haunts.

By dint of holding the gas canister in an inverted position and shaking
it vigorously every ten seconds a big spaghetti was prepared and
wolfed down. Then we retreated to the sleeping benches, lying close
for warmth, and very quickly dropped into deep dreams.

During our slumber, late into the night, a lone walker had arrived and
as he enjoyed a lie-in we secretly commandeered his stove to ensure a
quick hot brew before setting out into a hard frost – an underhand
action which roused pangs of guilt.

The sight from the doorway of Alder's scalloped flanks, with the
pointed Lancet Edge to its right confirmed the real joys of mountain
bothying. It held me in awe for a full minute despite the urge to get my
numbed toes and fingers moving. For Joy's part, she was visibly bright-
ening in the realisation that my extra stint yesterday meant that a
second night in this 'black hole' was obviated. Only the final summit
of the Aonach Beag chain, Carn Dearg, needed to be crossed and we
were left with the three Munros of the Ardverikie Forest, and a walk
out to Moy Lodge, our original schedule for a fourth day.

Crossing An Lairig from Carn Dearg we climbed Beinn a' Chlachair
by its steep east spur, a fine mixture of easy rock and ice work which
to my delight Joy found truly pleasurable. Up on its frosted summit
against the sweeping backdrop of Creag Meagaidh's many corries a
quite ridiculous scenario was enacted – husband and wife penning a
shopping list with gloved fingers before splitting company:

'Please don't forget a newspaper, and I'll meet you at 3.30,' I called
as she disappeared towards the distant Laggan road with a hitch-hike

to Fersit and a mad dash to Spean Bridge in prospect. Fetching the messages back home in Sheffield was never like this!

The Ardverikie district contains an extensive and imposing range of hills which would have been well suited for skiing had there been an unbroken snow cover. Instead, the route to Geal Charn was a tough plod. Where the snow was deeply drifted it strangely formed a bottom-less pit of sugary granules quite without cohesion. The puzzle of 'how?' occupied my attention for several minutes. Perhaps this was a 'depth hoar' formed when persistently low air temperatures create a steep heat gradient through the snow layers. It was, however, plainly obvious that a new fall of snow on top of this unstable mass would produce an unlimited avalanche potential.

Creag Pitridh was the last Munro of the group, merely a craggy eminence on Geal Charn's north-west shoulder and which by universal agreement is an unworthy member of the Tables. Despite the map's indication the summit is too abashed even to sport a cairn, one of only four Munros on which no man-made marker was found in the vicinity of the top.

The walk back to Moy Lodge was untowardly chilling. Once again exhaustion seemed to be catching up on me. But then with an uncanny telepathic timing, just as I crossed the bridge onto the main road Joy trundled along in the van, her remarkable speed saving me a frozen wait. In the back was a hoard of fresh groceries which ensured our self-sufficiency for a few days more.

Smooth unquestioning teamwork had seen us through Ben Alder Forest a day ahead of time and without a hitch or pitfall. But Joy's demand that night was: 'When are you going to take a complete rest day? You'll drive yourself into the ground if you're not careful.'

'How can I, as long as the weather stays like this?' I moaned.

The sustained bout of anticyclonic conditions was beginning to produce its own particular stress, namely a morbid fear of when the storms would arrive. In their absence I was risking a physical rundown by ploughing on so relentlessly.

How keenly I had looked forward to straddling the ridgetops of Glencoe in their full winter garb, and how disappointing that my brief days in the glen coincided with the only hiccups in this marvellous weather spell. My rearranged assignment with Alan Thomson on the Aonach Eagach was plagued by the passing of another weak front from the North Sea producing a light snowfall and shifting clouds conditions which were 'atmospheric' rather than 'photogenic':

> *Alan arrived an hour late with the lovely excuse that he thought we would*
> *want a long lie-in after our three days on Alder. I darkly suspected a heavy*
> *night at the Ballachulish bar! Nevertheless Joy and I were quickly*
> *organised for a series of shots in and around the van, and then I set off*
> *with him at a fair trot up Am Bodach which is the gateway to the 2 miles*
> *of pinnacles and knife-edges that constitute Scotland's most renowned*
> *mainland ridge. With a Munro at either end, I was committed to*
> *completing its whole.*

After a lengthy sequence of pictures on this first peak Alan returned to the road full of hope for the results, leaving me to continue alone, rather disoriented and off my guard. Such prolonged halts on the tops made me impatient and unsettled, especially the repeated stilted poses poised on the brink of the southern chasm which were enough to induce a mild attack of vertigo.

The instant one embarks onward from Am Bodach on the winter traverse true climbing terrain is encountered – an icy chimney, then the 'hogs-back' of The Chancellor which leads onto Meall Dearg, the first Munro, at 951m. Conditions on the ridge can vary enormously. Verglas on the rocks would be the least desirable. Today there was a light layer of fresh loose snow, and though the rocks beneath seemed dry, crampons were strapped on just in case there was any hidden ice. The main aid to route-finding hereabouts is indeed the scratchmarks on the rocks caused by scrattling crampon points.

An innumerable series of pinnacles links Meall Dearg to Sgurr nam Fiannaidh, the higher Munro at the western end. Over or round them? Always a vexing question on a 'gendarmed' crest, and one must be prepared to proceed by patient trial and error, never loath to retreat from blind alleys. Today the process was frustrating to me:

> *An experience I should have enjoyed was rather marred by the bad*
> *visibility and a jaded mood. Intermittently a window in the mist would*
> *open the excitingly precipitous drop to the green floor of the glen, but*
> *otherwise I wandered nonchalantly along, head in the clouds, and lacking*
> *the precise edge of control that I usually demand of myself when climbing*
> *unroped.*

Near the end, I passed two lads who were tortuously picking their way along in a series of roped pitches and abseils. Solo climbing is certainly faster but should be entertained only by the highly experienced. Better a late finish or even a benightment than a sorry rescue. The Aonach Eagach is a notorious venue for extended epics on account of its inescapability, and bobbing headlamps are often witnessed up on its crest long after darkness during the winter months.

Instead of the direct knee-grinding descent down the right side of the Clachaig Gully, a more subtle line using Fiannaidh's little south-eastern coire gave me a softer landing back on the Glencoe road. The invitation for tea, snacks and, most cherished of all desires, a hot bath, from Alan and his wife Ann was eagerly accepted. Already Alan had the contact sheets from today's films hanging up to dry, displaying an admirable professionalism that made me take proper regard of his solemn auguries of the pending storms.

Yet the forecast remained dry with the easterly airflow still dominant, and my thoughts were irresistibly drawn back to the west, to Glen Garry and Knoydart. Out towards the seaboard there would be minimal hindrance from the drifts which had proved so troublesome on Alder, and the Grampians and Cairngorms could be conveniently left until a heavier snowfall established better scope for skiing. To steal the Knoydart pack while conditions held would so strengthen my hand that three or four stormbound days could be withstood with indifference. But I also knew that these wild hills, of all Scotland's Munros, would not forgive an indiscretion.

We pulled up from a two and a half hour drive at the concrete bastions of Loch Quoich dam. The time for a change of mind had passed. I was committed to go, and nervously wrote:

Is this a rash move? Twenty miles, 9,000ft tomorrow and the roughest yet, heading alone for a bothy in the middle of nowhere, nine or ten miles from a roadhead, and inevitably arriving in pitch darkness. I fear I'm going to be running on empty. The prospect is alternately mouth-watering and spine-chilling!

6

ROUGH BOUNDS PASSAGE

14–18 January:
Glen Garry – Knoydart – Loch Lochy hills –
Loch Quoich group

The 1964 SMC Western Highlands Guide proclaimed that the ridge from Sgurr Mor to Sgurr na Ciche 'must be counted amongst the finest in the country. Not only is it narrow enough in places to provide a genuine mountaineering atmosphere, in hard winter conditions it demands care.' To this we were obliged to add its detached eastern outlier Gairich, 'the hill of roaring', its name a resonant clarion-call to hasten our approach on a dull and oppressive Monday morning, which could otherwise have easily killed the spirit. Up the long east ridge with a stalking path to help until the final rocky neck of the mountain, and out onto the snow-sheathed top – it is a long climb but well repaid by the sight of Loch Quoich slowly unfurling to its farthest reach.

We parted reluctantly. Joy retraced the route down to the dam, and took up a lonely watch for the day, which offered an ample opportunity to inform anxious parents of our movements:

> *From Gairich Martin has carried on into Knoydart on his biggest day yet.*
> *He is aiming for a bothy tonight, while I wait here by the foot of the loch in*
> *case he has to retreat. Tomorrow, on the assumption that he has pushed on*
> *to another bothy over his next two Munros, I will drive 15 miles to the*
> *head of the sea-loch and hike in 8 miles with extra supplies to meet him*
> *when he arrives. Then, weather permitting, we will do the last peak*
> *together on the third day, return to the bothy and walk back to the van. I*
> *hope this gives you some idea of what we are up to!!*

How reassuring it is to see your plans in writing. And I hardly think our families would have been much the wiser even had Joy interposed the missing placenames. Sourlies, Meall Buidhe, Luinne Bheinn, Kinloch Hourn, Barrisdale and Ladhar Bheinn is an obscure mouthful to inflict on most lowland Scots, never mind my Tyneside brood.

For myself, I swallowed the anguish of the 550m drop from Gairich and marched stoically up onto Sgurr an Fhuarain where the high road to Knoydart truly begins, and where sadly today the mists chose to draw their veil. My pace was steady not frantic, and twice delayed for nourishment – well judged, gauging from the smooth promenade over Sgurr Mor, Sgurr Beag and An Eag, to quit the mountain by nightfall. But then came Sgurr nan Coireachan, and a rude change of terrain. Simple ridge-trotting with warmly-pocketed hands switched to a mêlée of contorted outcrops destroying all directional awareness and enforcing many a scrambling detour. As I paused by the iron-speared final cairn the parting clouds briefly revealed the way ahead to Garbh Chioch Mhor. Commencing on the next bealach a black stone wall etched a snaking caterpillar up and over a host of slabs, dykes and towers to be lost finally in the haze somewhere about the summit.

Yet if the distant view was slightly daunting, in no way did it suggest the horrors of actually riding the crest, for it proved to be a real mountaineering rodeo. How a wall could be constructed in such a place confounds me yet. And to what purpose? But it exists as a lasting statue to hard skilled labour and the days when the whims of the landowners could be cheaply indulged, and as a firm companion to over an hour of torment:

> My time slipped, slid and then raced away. The drifted snow-banks to either side drove me to the despair of hopping along the top of the wall at many stages. At 4pm I staggered down onto the asylum of the Feadan na Ciche col, the toughest mountain of the trip finally vanquished, though not without a tooth-and-nail fight.
>
> And still the day's crowning peak, the terminal cone of Sgurr na Ciche, remained to climb. Leaving my sack by the wall but taking my headtorch lest night should fall I panted off up. A broad ramp slanting up to the left outwitted the rocky crest and in thirty-four breathless minutes I was back on the col, stealing only the shortest of stops on the top to peer into the clouded recesses of the Knoydart peninsula.

A joyous relief to have the ridge done welled up but was firmly brooked before it overflowed. Celebrations must wait until the tiny house of Sourlies, 900m below, was safely found.

Oh, for a full moon! The last light saw me down the boulder-choked cleft below the col but then all was blackness, without even a star to guide the descent. Steely sheets of ice underlay the bog-grass tussocks lower in the corrie. I would twist and turn around them until encir-cled, then attempt to skate an escape to the next dry island. From an especially bruising crash I stayed down on my back, flattened and for one painful minute wholly defeated. But as my breathing subsided the awesome silence of this West Highland night embraced my thoughts, softly whispering: 'Why despair? What matter another hour to the hut? Isn't this the land of your dreams? Calm down and keep your faith. It will soon be over!'

Such simple penetrating advice brought me back to my feet, and to a rational and hopeful renewal of effort. And indeed the misery was quickly ended. Tracking left out of the Allt Coire na Ciche and drop-ping between bare rock slabs, the Glen Dessarry path was met half-way down its serpentine descent from Mam na Cloich Airde. Twenty minutes later my torchlight picked out the squat shape of the bothy. My thoughts were still brimming with self-pity. Imagine then the shock of hearing merry voices babbling from within the walls, breaking the spell of solitude.

'My goodness, there must be some diehards around to want to come here on a January mid-week', I thought. The two inmates must have thought likewise, for they were no climbing vagabonds. Far from it; my night companions were married bank managers investing a precious week of their annual leave to seek a short adventure in the hills. 'Last winter we found the Cairngorms a bit crowded, so thought we'd try somewhere more remote' was their reasoning. Adding my chartered accountancy qualification onto their pile the three of us could have set up a finance bureau on the spot. So the day concluded with timely conviviality. One is never alone in one's madness!

Geographically, Knoydart is not entered until the River Carnach at the head of Loch Nevis is crossed. The aura of magic evoked by the name owes much to its difficulty of access. The occasional ferry from Mallaig to Inverie, a chartered boat from Arnisdale, or the treks from Kinloch Hourn and Dessarry: none is easy, and the overland entries are often plagued by heavy rains. A rain-gauge at the head of Loch Quoich recorded 44in of rainfall in January 1916. What price my chances had I chosen that year for my Munros venture? With the acres of bare rock exposed on the slopes, the direct run-off can approach 95 per cent in

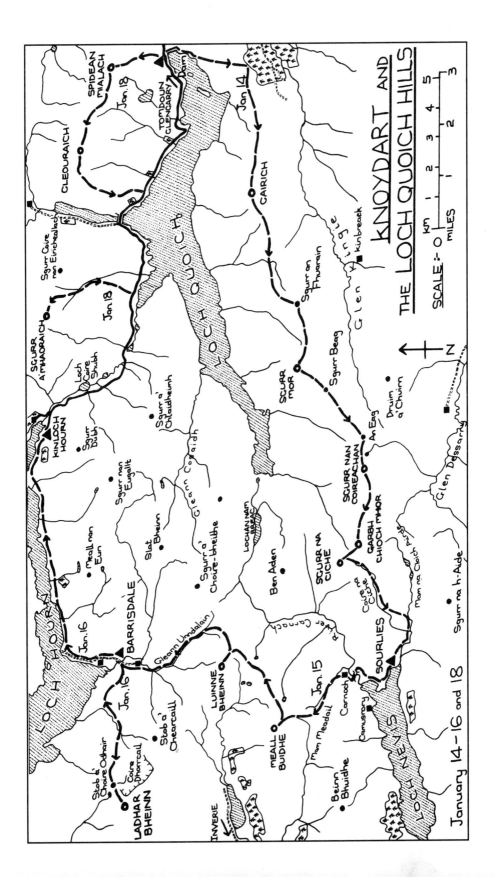

KNOYDART AND THE LOCH QUOICH HILLS

SCALE:-

km 0 1 2 3 4 5

MILES 0 1 2 3

N

January 14-16 and 18

SPIDEAN MIALACH

Jan 18

CLEOURAICH

TOM DOUN GLENGARRY

Jan 14

GAIRICH

Sgurr Coire nan Eiricheallach

Jan 18

Sgurr an Fhuarain

Glen Kingie

Kinbreack

SGURR A'MHAORAICH

Jan 18

Loch Coire Shubh

Sgurr Beag

SGURR MOR

Druim a'Chuirn

KINLOCH HOURN

Sgurr Dubh

Sgurr a'Chaorachain

Sgurr nan Eugallt

SGURR NAN COIREACHAN

An Eag

Glen Dessarry

Slat Bheinn

Gleann Cosaidh

GARBH CHIOCH MHOR

Mam na Cloich Airde

Sgurr na h-Aide

Meall nan Eun

Sgurr a'Choire-bheithe

Lochan nan Eag

Ben Aden

SGURR NA CICHE

Coire na Ciche

River Carnach

BARRISDALE

Jan 16

Jan 16

Gleann Unndalain

LUINNE BHEINN

SOURLIES

Stob a'Choire Odhair

Stob a'Chearcaill

Jan 15

Carnoch

Mam Meadail

LADHAR BHEINN

Coire Dhorrcaill

MEALL BUIDHE

Camasrory

INVERIE

Beinn Bhuidhe

LOCH NEVIS

LOCH HOURN

LOCH QUOICH

heavy storms, swelling dancing burns into raging torrents which can be impassable for many miles upstream.

The Carnach mudflats are especially prone to swamping owing to the tidal damming of the sea-loch, and the Sourlies bothy book recounts a host of aquatic epics in either reaching or quitting the peninsula. A new bridge over the river at Carnoch has partly allayed the challenge (or the danger, depending on your viewpoint) of the approach in recent years. Today the idea of being flooded seemed laughable, but sea-level frosts and winter droughts are quite exceptional here by the coast. And although we still shivered a little by the seaboard, the thermal effect of the Gulf Stream was keeping these western margins the warmest part of Europe in a spell that broke new records of frigidity on the Continent.

The seashore ambience burst refreshingly forth onto my senses as I left the hut in a clear dawn. The smell of salt air, and the cry of gulls here was another of Knoydart's attractions, the incomparable grandeur and variety of maritime mountains. Ciche's tapering cone sailed gracefully above the Carnach glen with the Garbh Chioch Mhor peeping sheepishly from behind. My appreciation of the pair was much improved in retrospect.

But the day's two Munros demanded the fullest attention, and such idle reflections were soon forgotten. On Mam Meadail an easterly wind sprang to life, and a ten-minute halt was required to struggle into 'longjohns'. The decision of whether to don extra underwear at the outset of the day is one which confounds the winter mountaineer. If the prejudgement of conditions is made wrongly (and it usually is) one suffers either heat exhaustion or frostbite, until forced to strip naked and reclothe, which is no picnic on an exiguous ledge or in a bitter gale.

> *Ominous cloudbanks appeared with the breeze. Was this the approaching blizzard? Meall Buidhe was a straight and simple haul from the Mam, but gave me sufficient excuse for an early lunch break. My last chocolate and biscuits disappeared with distressingly little effect. From here to Barrisdale there would be no more fuel.*

And beyond the twisted 2-mile ridge to Luinne Bheinn lay a sore trial of conscience in the guise of a potential Munro. The OS were up to their tricks again, raising Sgurr a'Choire-bheithe, the peak on the opposite side of Gleann Unndalain, from 913 to 914m in their new 1:25000 edition. This gave it a one-in-ten chance of being above 3,000ft which is 914.4m to the nearest point. The guardians of the Tables had written off for clarification but received the brusque reply that the OS no longer dealt in decimals, so the matter is left to be clarified by amateur surveyors*. My initial intention had been to 'knock it off' just to be sure, but now a host of reasons were found for its exclusion. Strictly one qualifies as a Munroist by completing all summits currently listed in the Tables. More pressingly, at that moment there was a big enough problem getting my carcass over Luinne Bheinn. The logic was indisputable. Original intent was quietly and gratefully ditched.

At least the snow clouds in the east broke rank and removed the fear of a storm, but I had little energy to spare on reaching the triple-topped summit of Luinne Bheinn, and sat down for a good rest and an early matinee of breathtaking views down to Barrisdale Bay and over to Ladhar Bheinn. It was a privilege to be there, the only spectator to Britain's finest and wildest land out of all her 50 million inhabitants.

A daylight descent was pure luxury after the happenings of the previous night. My worry now was not in reaching the bothy at Barrisdale, but how to replenish my famished and depleted resources to cope with Ladhar Bheinn on the morrow. To my eternal debt Joy was there to provide the solution:

Parking by the tiny jetty at Kinloch Hourn I shouldered a big load of fresh food, fuel and clothing, and embarked on the mule track which wended an undulating route above the lochside. As the loch broadened from its innermost arm, wonderful romantic views opened up, and the two-hour trek was a delight throughout. The last mile lay along by the seaweed and driftwood at the water's edge as I turned into Barrisdale Bay, passing a deserted lodge and disturbing a group of stags who were grazing around the bothy buildings.

As usual I entered with fear and trepidation, shouting 'hello' at the door and feeling stupid when I found it empty. A quick tour of inspection revealed ample potential to make this place 'home' for the night. There was a well appointed kitchen, a coal heap and bedrooms with fireplaces, plus a 'conscience box' for contributions. I gladly dropped some money in the tin and set about kindling a roaring fire.

Soup was already on the simmer when I spied Martin wandering down from the hills. He arrived looking chilled and dead-beat, his eyes glazed and hat askew, and promptly dived inside…

*

* It was subsequently confirmed that Sgurr a'Choire-bheithe is between 913.5 and 914m and therefore falls just short of 3,000ft.

Soup was succeeded by tea, fresh cheese omelette, carrots, garlic potatoes, then creamed rice and fresh fruit. The fire crackled gaily
throughout this three-hour feast, our legs stretched in front and bare
toes toasting with the heat, while tension unwound and spirits soared.
This was the perfect convalescence for the careworn climber.

The bothy is open to use by the public, thanks to the courtesy of the
estate keeper. One stupid act of vandalism could ruin this bond of trust
and it is to be sincerely hoped that every future habitué respects its
wonderful facilities. But the fear of abuse is not unwarranted. Knoydart
is certainly becoming popular in the summer months, for which the
bothy register evidenced a constant stream of visitors, including a
recent foray by Hamish Brown who had arrived by canoe from
Arnisdale and then ticked off *all* three Munros on the peninsula in a
single day, a feat which would have far eluded me in my present state.

With growing notoriety, the awareness of its unique and unspoilt
scenic value has raised the district to the forefront of environmental
concern. When the Knoydart estate was offered for sale in 1982 the
Ministry of Defence expressed a close interest in purchasing the area
for military training purposes, which would effectively bar all other
visitors and curb any further development of its crofting community
or indigenous industries. The idea provoked an outcry from conser-
vationists, but early the next year the scheme was quietly shelved
without any clear explanation.

However, the main conservation bodies, the Knoydart Foundation
and the National Trust, were themselves unable to formulate a co-ordi-
nated plan for its purchase, and the estate eventually fell to a private
bid from two Surrey property speculators. The initial ideas of this part-
nership for holiday homes and camps in the area caused no less suspicion and horror. However, their detailed proposals for 'timesharing'
ownership of parcels of land are in fact couched within close environmental constraints, so for the moment the protection lobbies are
breathing easy, and it is certain that exploitative schemes, which might
have proceeded unchecked twenty years ago when Knoydart was an
untrodden backwater, will never again be countenanced*.

---

* At the end of 1996 the majority of the Knoydart estate was again up for sale and prey
to the whims of private and corporate investors. However, a 3,000-acre parcel on the
north side of Ladhar Bheinn is safe. This was bought by the conservation group, the
John Muir Trust, in the mid-1980s.

As we snuggled down on the floorboards that night there was no sound save for the spitting of the waning fire and the scuttle of the resident mice.

What makes a truly 'great' mountain climb, an ascent that leaves one glowing with an unforgettable excitement? That of Ladhar Bheinn from Barrisdale possesses every required ingredient. There must first exist the mystique of the unknown and the unseen. From the bothy one discerns just enough of the mountain's subsidiary spurs and spires to attract yet not reveal. In particular the turret of Stob a'Chearcaill rears up its head in bold defiance as if to shield a wealth of hidden cliffs. Of course, the approach should quicken the interest as well as display a charm and beauty in its finer detail, and the winding stalker's track up into Coire Dhorrcail fulfils these demands admirably, relinquishing the seashore to be gradually absorbed into high mountain terrain.

Then, and most crucially, the revelation of the crowning peak and the climb to its summit need to be direct and stunning. As the savage array of cliffs and chasms at the head of the corrie meets the forward gaze at a sudden turn in the path the upwards urge becomes truly uncontainable. These mica-schist precipices reach in excess of 300m in vertical height, and in a hard winter have an impressive potential. However, the approach is long and conditions so prone to freakish change that only the patient and dedicated have staked a claim up there. In 1962 the irrepressible Aberdonian pioneer Tom Patey climbed the first significant routes which were not appreciably augmented until 1978 when the visits of Con Higgins, Andy Nisbet and friends raised the standards to grades IV and V.

The top lies on the right of the coire, and is airily gained over the knife-edge arête of Stob a'Choire Odhair. The icy and viciously gusty conditions which we met on the ridge were enough to deter Joy from continuing but provided me with an exhilarating finale. Muffled up in hood, balaclava and double mittens the blast could be faced with impunity, although the flutters of snowflakes racing past brought back an undercurrent of anxiety. And the summit itself? An elegant edge of snow is capped with three neat pikes to ice the cake.

Ladhar Bheinn well deserves such extended praise, but perhaps it commits a despicable sin to put this in print, tearing aside the cloak of secrecy which has kept the mountain inviolate. Given ten years we might see its demise under a plethora of cairns and signposts, erosion scars and scree runs. Along with praise the peak deserves respect, and one can only plead with all who go to leave no mark of passage.

By 1.30 we were back at the bothy, and after a hot drink bade goodbye to Barrisdale. Joy relived each step of the walk by Loch Hourn as my animated guide, proudly pointing out each new view and feature as the track unfolded. Yet there was relief in seeing the van on rounding its final turn. The enclosed trough of Kinloch Hourn would so easily have trapped us had the snows come, for the road escapes to Loch Quoich only by a tortuous climb of 200m. And it was doubly comforting to get down to the sheltered woods of Glen Garry where we halted that night, for Knoydart in winter leaves a lonely print in the memory.

Next morning there was smug satisfaction and celebration to see low cloud and a fine drizzle that was surely falling as snow not far above our parking height of 150m. We had beaten the weather, but only just, and several easier options were now at our disposal. Number one in Joy's mind was a rest day for me. My revival at Barrisdale was no more than a short pause in an overall physical decline and the mental strain was now so insistent that sleep was coming only with difficulty.

There was no personal precedent to guide a decision. Twenty-seven days without a break was far beyond my previous experience, but the exploits of others could possibly give some guidance. However much I had admired the Himalayan run of the Crane brothers, their initial tactics were primitive and almost fatal. Setting out in a mood of 'do or die' they piled on the agony for seventeen days of non-stop effort, until ground to exhaustion during a headlong dash from Everest Base Camp to Kathmandu. Demoralised, close to abandoning the attempt, and prey to illness, especially dysentery, they barely made any further advance for the next week, and only by calling upon remarkable powers of recovery were able to complete their triumph at a slightly more modest pace. Their salutary experience was not lost on the staff of Intermediate Technology, and Steve Bonnist often reminded me of the proverb 'slow and steady wins the race', for the 'Summits for Survival' appeal depended totally on my ultimate success.

However, in every accountant there is a tidy mind and an exasperating obsession to balance the books and rule off, so I could not have rested easy until the Garry and Quoich hills were complete. Joy knew well when argument was pointless, but vehemently branded me as an incurable 'head banger', before acceding to my day's scheme – a short jaunt from Laggan Locks to the two Munros above Loch Lochy.

We stopped at Invergarry post office en route, eager to see whether Alan Thomson's photos had achieved due acclaim in the national press; but no, our faces did not grace that day's edition, and yesterday's had all been sold or returned. Yet the proprietor surveyed us with a penetrative stare that brought a happy sequel two days later. When we called again by chance for stamps and milk, his wife casually asked us: 'Wis it you in here asking for old newspapers during the week?' and on our confirmation promptly produced the desired cuttings from *The Scotsman* and *Press and Journal*.

'They don't miss a trick these Highlanders', whispered Joy. Yet what thoughtfulness to have sought out the copies on the slim possibility of our return. And of course her disclosure precipitated a lively and prolonged conversation. Once the reserve of the local people was breached, their warmth to us was unlimited.

The 'Lochy hills' are a compact chain of summits but lack the bare ferocity of the peaks further west, and only at two points, Meall na Teanga and Sron a'Choire Ghairbh, reach over 3,000ft. As always we approached by the quickest route possible, tramping along the roads of South Laggan Forest and up the track to Cam Bhealach from where the Munros are immediately accessible.

Indeed it was snowing steadily above 300m, and drifting on the higher slopes, but conditions were severe rather than atrocious, grade 4 on the 1 to 6 scale which I had devised to classify their daily fluctuations through the season. Grade 6 would denote a storm-force blizzard, when I would be best tucked up inside the van.

Our descent passed through a forest patch where industrious felling operations were in full swing. Diesel-powered winches and pulleys assisted the labour but Joy was quick to observe as we passed the drenched group of loggers: 'I only hope they're getting paid well working in conditions like this.'

Yet I wonder on their comments on a pair of volunteers like ourselves. 'Bloody crazy!' I should imagine.

The five-hour round was as much as could be managed today, and it was difficult for me to handle the various tasks during our subsequent visit to Fort William, especially a radio interview for the *Good Evening Scotland* programme, on which for once my weary grunts and groans were quite authentic.

Once familiar, 'the Fort' is a warm and friendly town, and does not deserve the verbal slanging to which it is regularly subjected by tourists who search for Disneyland perfection in their resort. The place makes no pretensions to beauty and it bustles with a life both seemly and unsavoury. Long-term unemployment and the abject resignation of its victims are to be seen as well as happy indulgence and thriving business. It cuts a vivid slice across the state of modern Britain. The visit was especially welcome following our seclusion out west, but by 8pm we were back in our preferred haunt – the soft woods by Tomdoun.

At 1am I was wide awake and ferretting about the van like a bothy mouse. A cup of hot chocolate and an hour's reading later I drifted reluctantly back to sleep.

'My body-clock has gone haywire, this will definitely be my last day', I declared over breakfast.

Only the three big hills on the north side of Loch Quoich separated me from that vital rest, but was I capable of making 1,980m (6,500ft) and 13 miles in the day?

The weather was bright and breezy at Quoich dam, and bitter and blustery 760m higher on top of Spidean Mialach. The snowstorm had passed on without decisive impact, and still the dry easterlies blew, rushing through the col to Gleouraich at gale force and whisking plumes of powder snow high into the air. They rendered the buffeted crawl to the summit every bit as thrilling as the final steps to a Himalayan giant. Like a yacht caught in a storm I tacked between the southern ridges, trading drifted lee for blasted foreslope, then slid down the grasses to the road where Joy was stationed after a direct descent from the Spidean and a short drive with the van.

Split days on the hill brought a problem which centred squarely on the reclining lunch break. After soup and oatcakes and a couple of crumpets you feel so nicely attuned to the lunchtime radio that even *The Archers* makes palatable listening, and the immediate attraction of Sgurr a'Mhaoraich, the third fine peak of the Quoich trilogy, quickly loses its appeal. But towards 2pm we took the van across the bridge which spans the loch's long northern inlet, and made tentative motions back towards the great outdoors. My morning elation evaporated, and feeling like a tin kettle boiled dry I immediately fell into Joy's foot-steps, and trailed behind her all the way up Coire nan Eiricheallach and onto the top. It was definitely the time to cry 'enough'! Joy herself was amazed at my dismal abdication of the route-finding role.

Summit vistas, as so often in recent days, were obscured by a light cloud capping. We waited for fifteen minutes with camera shutter poised but not a chink of view emerged. I could tread most of these hills a second time yet see them as new.

Mhaoraich was one of many mountains in the district which bore the fleeing steps of Prince Charlie in the months after Culloden. He sneaked past a line of English sentries at Loch Coire Shubh and escaped to Glen Shiel by Coire Sgoireadail on the western slopes. The prince's game of cat and mouse with the Redcoats has written one of the most romantic episodes in the history of the Western Highlands, and establishes him as a mountaineer of considerable calibre, for he was forced to stay high and live rough for many weeks as he awaited tidings of ships to France.

Emotion rose close to the surface as we drove away from Quoich for the last time to a third night's stay at Tomdoun. Ninety-nine Munros was hardly the most desirable number on which to pause. They had occupied 29 days, a total of 375 miles and ascent of 53,030m (174,000ft). By compressing two days into one on Alder and in Lochay, and skipping a statutory rest day, I was fully three up on schedule. But above all this, there was a humble gratitude for my good fortune just to be there, right in the midst of the struggle.

7

BLIZZARD OVER KINTAIL

19–22 January:
The Cluanie Ridge and The Saddle –
The Brothers and Sisters of Kintail

Moving north from Glen Garry the ever-rolling West Highland chain folds dramatically into Glen Shiel, and it is here that the Munros' population reaches its greatest density, no fewer than twenty flanking the Road to the Isles as it snakes its famous path from the Cluanie watershed down the 8-mile glen to Loch Duich. And behind these immediate ridges lies a tempting host of more reclusive peaks.

This array of nearby summits makes the Cluanie Inn an incomparable centre for a mountain walking holiday for it is sited magnificently at their focal point; and the hotel returns the compliment of its location in full measure, exemplifying the traditional warmth and quality of the Highland coaching house, its panelled walls steeped in centuries of travelling history. It was by the inn that we drew up our modern-style coach towards the end of that precious day of rest that all too predictably had disappeared in a flash, and ironically flowered into one of the season's loveliest – tranquil, sunny and laden with dew. So rapid was its passage that I wondered how it could succeed in recouping the strength that was now required to traverse the southern side of the glen. Logically, our route was moving north until the long-awaited blizzards arrived, an event so far postponed that we might yet reach Ben Hope before turning to skis and the eastern hills.

The day proposed not only spanned the Cluanie Ridge but continued over Sgurr na Sgine to The Saddle, and so would complete one of Britain's longest high-level traverses, for this multi-peaked roller-coaster never falls below 650m throughout its 10-mile length. The Cluanie Ridge itself gives seven Munros and an oft walked edge of

This ridge was our unanimous choice but its pleasure was spoilt by another moping morning. However Martin Stone is always bubbling with bright-eyed schemes for future marathons, and at the foot of the spur reminded us that we now stood on the watershed of Britain. The indeterminate mass of peaty channels by which we were encircled hardly seemed the spot for such a historic declaration, but of course he was correct. To our right the Abhainn Gaorsaic now gathered every pool and runnel, stealthily amassing volume and strength in its 5-mile meander, to spout forth in a single 110m drop over the Falls of Glomach and speed away to Loch Long and the western seas. And yet the crucial point of birth of such a stupendous torrent is a barely perceptible bog. The Western Highlands watershed repeats this pattern throughout its length, being dissected by east-west glacial breaches which bear the waters in both directions from low summits.

But to return to Martin, the purpose of his revelation was far from geographical tuition, but rather to tell us about his planned 'British watershed walk' which would follow the precise divide between the North Sea and the Atlantic from Caithness south to Land's End.

'I've traced the route on all the maps, it's the last great challenge', he pronounced.

Well, maybe; but while the straths and bens of Scotland would make a superb setting for its initial stage perhaps the shine might have worn off by the time you are crawling through canal ducts in the middle of Birmingham. No doubt it will be done though.

The link from Fhada to A'Ghlas-bheinn is disrupted by the precipitous gap of Bealach an Sgairne which is one of the principal ports of entry to the Affric wilderness. We spent some time searching a means of access from above, and settled finally on a safe northwards detour. A'Ghlas-bheinn is then gained by an ever-rising series of knolls, which put one in mind of Haystacks, the Lakeland favourite.

As we strolled back towards Affric with shirt sleeves rolled up in a drier afternoon it left me uneasy that these fell-men might be thinking my exploit just a little soft. For after all they probably *ran* the 12 miles of this walk every day at home! But Pete's thoughts were at that moment quite the reverse:

> *The day was the most sociable of all; I just wished this lifestyle could go on. But jealousy is a futile emotion – I've had my chances and stuck with the safer income of the city. But these days will be long remembered – time to*

enjoy the hills, to walk with a different person on every stretch and talk on a closer personal level...

For me there was even time to take an hour's sleep before dinner. Harder days lay ahead but I emerged from this cure feeling a new man.

Planning for the final day in Affric was another game of chess. At least the transport was in place down the glen and my route of egress already settled along the northside ridges from Mam Sodhail to Toll Creagach, 18 miles and 1,950m (6,400ft) by the map. However, everyone naturally wanted the chance to walk the tops, especially as the skies were clearing and the breeze swinging back to the east to bring a return of frost; but unfortunately there were several tasks to share such as cleaning out the hostel and portering three substantial loads down to the road.

The most admirable quality of the fell-running fraternity, apart from their hardiness, is a spirit of mutual support. The foursome had no self-seeking motive in being here. Their stated job was 'to help me over' whatever Munros I chose, and they had displayed unquestioning deference to my every preference on route, pace and timing. This is their customary style. Each member of a club will take his due turn in the limelight whilst his mates give total commitment to help him achieve his challenge.

And now there was no hint of rancour as the 'straws were drawn'. Joy was not allowed to stand down. 'No; you must have the day with Martin', they protested, appreciating that this was a rare opportunity for her to relinquish her own supporting role. Martin Stone drew the lucky lot to join us. Pete and Chris would ferry loads, but make a short dash to the highest peaks en route, while Roger cleaned the hut and took the biggest sack directly back, willingly taking on the least glamorous job of all.

Bathed in pinky sunlight the snow-streaked hills bore the freshness of an Alpine spring this morning. We three took a rising traverse from the valley floor and then kicked up the sequinned snows of Coire nan Each to debouch on Mam Sodhail's southern spur, as the sunlight spread into its fullest radiance. There could be no doubt about the weather:

I knew I was lucky. The average winter may produce ten such days so I could count my share already, and here was February hardly begun...

Mam Sodhail and Carn Eige used to confuse me as a lad. At 1,180 and 1,183m they are the highest peaks west of the Great Glen, but each atlas or touring map would name one and not the other in identical location, leaving me under the delusion that they were the same mountain. The twin rooftops of the west are in fact only three-quarters of a mile apart, and though Eige is just the higher, Mam Sodhail was preferred as a major station in the Principal Triangulation of the British Isles and so is named on maps with equal frequency. On its summit we took our snack by the remnant of the stone tower which was constructed in the 1840s to assist the survey. Originally 7m tall, it is still an impressive monument at its present height of 3m.

Carn Eige's conquest was deferred until we had visited the northern offshoot of Beinn Fhionnlaidh, which has a status parallel to that of Mullach na Dheiragain though is not so far removed from its parent peak. Both these outliers overlook the deserted head of Loch Mullardoch, facing directly my hills of tomorrow.

By happy chance we met Chris and Pete on Carn Eige summit and lunched together. In all these four days we had the hills to ourselves. The ongoing ridge has some slender sections as far as Tom a'Choinich, with fine northern exposures over Coire Domhain, but thereafter slowly casts aside its armour to finish tamely on the rounded dome of Toll Creagach, the fifth and final Munro. Mam Sodhail has a parallel but shorter eastern arm which contains the Top of Sgurr na Lapaich. Viewed both from our own highway just to the north and especially from the lower glen, Lapaich possesses sufficient aplomb to be accorded the sixth full Munro of the range. The combined circuit of these two ridges would make the centrepiece of any Affric trip.

From Creagach we dropped directly southwards into the afforested hearth of the lower glen. Yes; perhaps this is Scotland's most lovely. The wooded mix of ancient pine and modern fir is intertwined to a velvet luxuriance, and its rich fragrance reached up to draw us off the frosted tops. We were loath to go inside once down and stood by the van vacantly gazing over the orange millpond of the river until the sun was lost.

Sadly, our companions' stay was now concluded. Four hundred mindless miles of motorway to drive tonight, and by 9am tomorrow they would be back in front of office desks and computer screens. The thought aroused no trace of envy. My accountant's hat had been hung up long ago. When we had all regathered Joy and I made a large fresh meal to fuel their journey which we hoped would be a small gesture of thanks for their fine support.

The northern ridge of Glen Cannich from Carn nan Gobhar over Sgurr na Lapaich to An Socach vies with that of Affric for height and continuity – such similar groups of hills yet with wholly different impact on successive days. At first the absence of company was keenly sensed. No human buffer was there to shield the stark loneliness of these empty hills; and then there was the glowering weather. Under a blanket of leaden cloud and in a biting easterly wind, today's thin crests exuded only menace. And to complete the change, my strides today were ever westward bound, each summit one more step from the Cannich roadend until at An Socach only the wilderness expanse of Killilan Forest lay in front. There is no sanctuary over there for a dozen miles, and Glen Cannich's woods were fully nine behind me:

> At times I wished myself in the shops of Inverness with Joy, but then thought better of such envy for here my chosen battle was right at hand steering my compass through every turn of An Riabhachan's 2-mile crest, then seeking its vital western exit down the shrouded rocky scarp below. Inside my mittens my finger-ends were still frozen white, making the final link to An Socach a trial of endurance. Clench them, shake them – 100… 200 times – keep the blood flowing…

The crowning trig on Socach was touched, then fled. A tingling warmth returned down in the sheltered folds of Coire Mhaim, but the long trek back remained.

This punishing walk towards nowhere formed the final act of the Affric scheme, and was certainly its least attractive portion. But the only shorter means of access to the ridge would have been a camp at the head of Mullardoch, set up on completion of the Ceathreamhnan traverse, an exciting thought but risky in its logistics. So having chosen instead to make the Lapaich group a one-day circuit I now set my head square into the wind for a gruelling return beside the gloomy loch.

Mullardoch, Monar, Cluanie and Quoich – these four great waters have all been dammed and raised for hydro-electric power production and in the doing their pre-existent nets of tracks have been disrupted. On Mullardoch as much can be sensed from a glance at the map. Zigzag tracks career off the tops to plunge into the waters, sometimes re-emerging several miles further down the shores. New walking thoroughfares have sadly not been established. The stalkers wisely now prefer a boat to get to the upper reaches, which gave little consolation as I ploughed between the remnant paths.

The loch was the most sombre of all the wild places seen on my travels. It evokes deep sadness and powerful inspiration on a brooding day like this. One thinks of all the woes and trials of Highland history; only the mournful skirl of the pipes is lacking, but there are no people here to listen. Not even in summer would a piper be paid his worth. It left me craving warmth and company, and comfort too, for the wind had sapped all strength. At 4.15 I rounded the final headland and passed the boat houses and jetty. But though Joy was waiting by the terminal dam with her glowing complexion and a flood of news, it was all too hard to grasp, still less respond, in my tired and humbled state.

Strathfarrar is the third of the big glens between the Shiel and Carron. Its private road meanders with the river for a dozen miles of sylvan charm as far as the Monar dams. Up above them the steely sheet of the loch snakes west for 10 miles more. Five wild Munros lie about the West Monar Forest at its upper end, but being nearer to Strathcarron than the Farrar roadend these would be left for the later Torridonian campaign. But just north of the lower glen is a further ring of four summits which were a brief finale to this present phase of western exploration.

The estate restricts public access via the road to daylight hours, and then the numbers of vehicles are closely controlled:

Having sensibly arranged permission from the factor by phone last night we took a couple of hours' extra sleep and made a late start up the glen at 9.30. By approaching first the easternmost peak of Sgurr na Ruaidhe once again the wind was behind us on the tops. In today's strong breeze this really felt like cheating, and with the snows frozen to rock-hard consistency we fair flew over Carn nan Gobhar. Yesterday's clouds had lifted and the air and views were invigorating, especially down over Beauly and the Moray lowlands. While Joy went down to the van from Sgurr a'Choire Ghlais, I collected the last Munro, Sgurr Fhuar-thuill, then ran down the Allt Toll a'Mhuic with the help of a good track to meet the road by Inchvuilt. These rounded friendly hills had taken just 4 hours and 20 minutes, and I still felt fresh and buoyant. In fact I'm right on top of my game, now four days up on schedule with 167 done in 49 days. Maybe now I can take the Cairngorms in a single bite and put the issue beyond doubt.

This burst of euphoria, despite its bravado, can claim justification remembering the real trepidation on setting out from Cluanie six days previously. This vast forest of high hills had elicited my greatest respect, and to complete their summits without hitch or delay was an unexpected boon. Which is not to say that the area failed to match its imagined reputation. The three glens – Affric, Cannich and Farrar – in their lower parts are the most enchantingly beautiful that we saw, yet each has birth in an upper reach of awesome wildness. And the summit ridges can fulfil what must be every mountain walker's dream – to stride unfettered over narrow crests for day upon day without foreseeable end, a master to all he beholds.

11

IN BLEAKEST MIDWINTER

8–16 February:
Feshie – Tilt, Shee and Clova – Lochnagar –
Mount Keen

The air was thick with dust and grit, gathered up into spiral clouds, then flung full length across our tracks. Only a skin of ice still clung to the ground, and the booming wind echoed round the corrie. Each blast would send us skidding backwards clawing for a rock to hold. There was no hope without crampons. Grasping vainly at the flying straps with mittened hands, our minds too numbed to tie the knots properly, the job of fitting them took ten minutes. Helping each other to our feet we staggered forward...

All this, and we hadn't even left the car park! Coire Cas on Cairn Gorm – one day the skier's sunny paradise, the next a bowl of white hell. Yet even this morning there were a few brave souls scattered over the nursery slopes, loath to admit defeat despite the frank impossibility of standing up in balance. But for me there was no point in persevering against insuperable odds. The simple climb to Cairn Gorm summit would have asked my all, never mind the planned continuation to Bynack More, and at this stage if a scheduled route could not be met then energies might as well be saved for tomorrow.

The White Lady Shieling was far enough to say we'd tried without getting into trouble. We retreated inside its deserted restaurant for a minute's breather before going back, glad of a secure shelter or so we thought. But not even the shieling was immune to the power of the storm. During the following night it burnt to the ground, due to a tiny wall fire fuelled and fanned by the rising gale. Had we bought a cup of tea we might have been the last customers.

Yesterday's plan for a four-day swoop on the area's seventeen

Munros was but a fond memory, and even today's idea of doing the northernmost two now a tattered banner. After I had respectfully jock-eyed around them for the last three weeks why did the Cairngorms have to smite me in the face on the very day I took my battle there?

That night as the storm reached its zenith we sheltered in the pinewoods by Glenmore Lodge. The skies were a clear pale blue at dawn, but looking over to Cairn Gorm, the plateau was shrouded in the same purple cloud that had accompanied yesterday's hurricane. These lenticular or 'fisheye lens' clouds are a sure sign of turbulence on the tops. The access road to the ski-roads was blocked by the blown snow, yet despite all this we tuned to the radio to hear these fairy-tale pronouncements:

'Mountain weather for the Cairngorms: sunny intervals and scattered snow showers, wind south-east fresh to strong...'

'Ski-reports: Cairn Gorm: main runs all complete, vertical runs 1,800ft, wide snow cover, surface icy...'

Anyone sitting at home in Glasgow listening to those bright and breezy predictions might have been half-way to Aviemore at the time we gave up hope and drove round to Glen Feshie (see map on page 142). Not even the specialist forecasts are able to assess the remarkable local intensity of a Cairngorm storm. The gentle plateau topography welcomes any south-easterly airstream with open arms, giving a perfect take-off board from which the convergent winds jet down the northern corries at a destructive velocity. It is sound advice to double the quoted windspeed and stay off these hills when a sou-easter is in flow in winter.

But sitting in lower Glen Feshie, bathed in sun and seeing only a soft breeze at play in the treetops, it was still hard to accept defeat, and furthermore, two full days without progress would cut my hard-won lead by half. What if gales kept up for a week? The final straw was to see a party of middle-aged ramblers set off up the track from Achlean towards the Carn Ban Mor. They were probably going nowhere near the tops, but my pride was sufficiently pricked that I followed their suit at 2pm.

Sgor Gaoith was the aim, the higher of the 'Sgoran' twins which over-look the head of Glen Einich in a 2-mile barrier of cliffs. The approach from Feshie is a simple stroll, but for chance of meeting that cliff-edge in a white-out, a serious undertaking. Only a lucky clearance in the cloud on the approach gave me the slightest hope of safely finding the summit. Whenever the shroud was drawn the surface drift of the snow produced the mesmeric effect of a moving quicksand. All sense of balance, slope and direction was destroyed. Even free of cloud it took a tense half hour to find the precipice and skirt its edge to the highest point. Because the top is unmarked, back-bearings, map-sections and other navigational tricks were employed to prove it, using the gloomy sheet of Loch Einich below as the only sure reference point.

The sortie had hardly brought a rich reward for all its risk, but in a war of attrition, no summit would yield easily.

The storm was recharged in energy come the start of its third day, wiping out every hope other than to struggle up the other Feshie Munro, Mullach Clach a'Bhlair. Joy sensed my desolation and joined the fight.

Without permission to drive on the private road up the west side of the river, Achlean farm was the nearest starting point. A sheltered valley approach to a full-blown tempest is if anything worse than the battle up top, and so it was on the 2-mile trudge to Carnachuin:

> The pasting that was coming to us was all too clear from the headwind
> funnelling down the glen. Despite the bitter cold I was sweating with
> apprehension. Every little discomfort, the rub of the boot, my streaming
> nostrils, or the whip crack of the wind in my hood, was saying 'give in and
> go back' ...

But once the first steps upward were made this sickly fear and cowardice vanished entirely. I was heartily glad of the broadly bull-dozed track which led us up almost onto the summit plateau where it was lost under the snowfields, for once forgetting my dislike of such scars on the land.

Our objective stands at the south-west corner of the Moine Mhor, or Great Moss, the moorland expanse which marks the western bound of the Cairngorms range. Originally five Munros lay in close proximity to the Moss, barely decipherable on the criterion of 'separate mountains', but since 1974 three have been rightly demoted to Tops to leave Sgor Gaoith and this Mullach of today as the definitive hills of the area.

On the final steepening the wind threw itself upon us. There was no cloud as such, only a 10m cowl of blowing snow through which a blue sky was occasionally glimpsed, but once enclosed within its wrap:

... I could only recall the 20,320ft summit of Mount McKinley in Alaska for a proper comparison to the severity of these conditions – gusts of 80 or 90mph blowing us over, and a wind-chill temperature below the minus thirty mark with real frostbite potential. Behind me Joy's face was masked by a cake of frozen breath which had grown between her trails of hair. We took turns to break the wind, making quick dashes forwards in the clearer lulls until the paltry pile of summit stones was found... And oh, the relief of getting back to the glen with its stands of pine, farms and cottages – so welcome now that we had survived our task.

After the ethereal splendour of the morning, our later visit to the Aviemore Centre was quite inappropriate. Its concrete façades and manufactured entertainments made us wonder which indeed was the alien world. We bought a paper and commiserated with the groups of would-be skiers who mooched around the lifeless precincts, then left to soothe our worries by the frozen shores of Loch Morlich. Two simple summits which one could be round in four hours of good weather had soaked up three whole days. What next was in store?

The curtain rose brightly on day four, everywhere at least except the Cairn Gorm plateau. All ready in boots and gaiters, and with flask and sandwiches packed, we drove up Glen More confident at last of doing the Cairn Gorm–Bynack round. Yet to our infuriated despair as soon as the forest opened up, there were the same stormclouds covering the tops, and the ski-road was still blocked, precipitating an urgent dilemma. To risk waiting could mean the loss of another day and the onset of total demoralisation, yet time was short to go elsewhere.

On decisive impulse we drove off at full throttle over Drumochter to Blair Atholl. Cairn Gorm was handed its just victory, but surely the central Grampians would be more tolerant of our presence. The forecast was optimistic. Atlantic and Scandinavian airmasses had been tightly wedged over northern Britain in the last three days but now were disengaging from their tussle, and a gradual moderation of the wind could be expected. At Atholl a minor road turns left from Bridge of Tilt and climbs steeply to the open braes by Monzie farm. At 9.45am it was late already.

From here for 20 miles north and east to Glen Dee lies the heart of the Grampian chain, an empty moorland deserted by the finer touch of Nature's brush, abundant only in its barrenness, and under winter's snows enough to sink the strongest spirit. So great is the expanse that

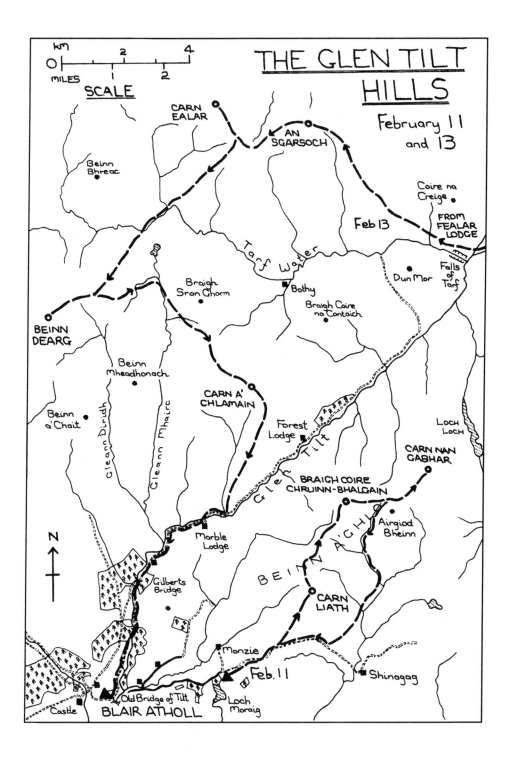

it completely fills the 'Braemar' Ordnance Survey sheet. With the maps spread out, the eye is arrested less by the summits of the area than the meandering watershed lying at its centre between the Geldie, Tilt and Feshie catchments, their discordant drainage evidencing major glacial interference. The rivers Tilt and Feshie captured parts of the head-waters of the Geldie, which were blocked by glaciers in the main Dee valley during the Ice Age. Each has since carved a lower gorge of impressive depth, but left the Geldie bereft of erosive power. The linkage of the three glens enables through treks to be undertaken between Braemar, Badenoch and Atholl, which are lengthy but very popular in summer.

Only one mountain group stands aloof from these arguing waters: Beinn a'Ghlo, the highest ground of the Grampians save for Lochnagar, and a steeply sculpted mass of rounded tops and three Munros. In our disorganisation it formed the only close objective for a day's round trip, travelling over the summits from Carn Liath to Carn nan Gabhar and descending by the eastern flanks towards Shinagag until a farm track leads back west to Monzie.

Joy watched me set off in full expectancy of a hard struggle and a late return, but conditions aheight were unsavoury rather than murderous, and no real hindrance to progress. At last the storm had eased its grip. The snow was confined to the lee-slopes, where it had been set like cement by the wind, giving a quick approach, and on finishing the trio a running descent down the drifted course of the western stream of Airgiod Bheinn was possible. The following traverse to the Shinagag track was a contrasting slog in knee-deep heather. All the way along a 'snowcat' vehicle shadowed my steps, bringing the fear that it was stalking *me* rather than the hinds which are culled during the winter months. However, it finally passed on the track with a pair of beasts strapped to the sides, the bodies lifeless yet still steaming from the heat of their final flight.

That evening we entertained a distinguished visitor from the colon-nades of Fleet Street. We were viewing the press suspiciously, knowing that all publicity would help the charity but fearing that glorified reporting would demean our enterprise to the level of a stunt with ourselves as a pair of performing puppets. 'Tough Training for Bonington!' was one typically silly headline that followed our capers on Creag Meagaidh. However, we were instructed by IT to be on our very best behaviour tonight, for our guest, Mike Herd, was the sports feature writer for the prestigious *London Evening Standard,* and so intrigued on hearing of our doings that he had made a special journey to investigate. From both stature and dress it was clear that his avid love for sport was safely couched in the armchair, and his swift removal from Pitlochry's four-star Atholl Palace Hotel into our sweaty cabin for dinner came as a rude shock. Yet he displayed a delightful charm and interest throughout the ordeal, even expressing the hope of taking a little air with us on the morrow at Glen Shee.

There are two further groups of Munros in the vicinity of Glen Tilt, a string of eight beginning on The Cairnwell summit, and the ring of four around the Tarf Water to the west of the main glen. Each group would give an arduous day of nigh on 25 miles with perforce an overnight bivouac between, somewhere in the glen's upper reaches. Here as nowhere else the Nordic skis were needed, but without continuous snow there was no choice but to go on foot, and quickly too.

A start was made from Cairnwell to use the 665m height advantage of Scotland's highest road pass. Tomorrow's route would finish back at Blair Atholl, so Joy could not be with me for need of moving our transport; and more was the pity, for this is the sort of country where company is at a premium.

Mike came up Glen Shee to see me off. No amount of persuasion would take him ten paces off the chairlift car park. After briefly sniffing the chilly morning air, he wished us well, dived into his car and hastened back to breakfast at the Palace. Yet our antics left a suitable impression for he wrote a most entertaining article to our favour which must have left many a Cockney commuter scratching his head in wonder.

On a bleak midwinter morning the rim of the Glen Shee pistes from Carn Aosda to The Cairnwell is the edge of civilisation. Below, hordes of skiers are already disgorging from cars and buses and rapidly turning the slopes into ant-hills, whilst over to the west is an unbroken desert, imported direct from the Arctic tundra. An Socach, Glas Tulaichean, Beinn Iutharn Mhor, Carn an Righ – they are all obscured by a haze of merging snow and cloud. The foreground plane of mottled moor is powdered white, blotched by peat, and destitute of form and feature. One searches for a gauge of scale, and maybe a twisting clough or shooter's box is spotted, but is it one, two or three miles away? Even map and compass are confused, and slow to give the answer. All this

THE STANDARD

Monday, February 18, 1985   20p   *Incorporating the* **Evening News**

MARTIN and JOY MORAN . . . sold their house and took to the high road.

Moran's theme: Climb every mountain . . .

MICHAEL HERD reports

SIR HUGH MUNRO probably didn't know what he was starting best part of a century ago when he painstakingly mapped and listed the 277 Scottish peaks that are more than 3000 feet high.

Since 1891, the year in which the worthy knight completed his task, the Munros, as they have become known, have been a target for British mountaineers. Some men have made it their life-time objective to climb the lot and three have actually scaled all 277 in one spring-summer season. But no-one has succeeded in reaching every peak in a winter.

Some climbers have thought of it and abandoned the idea as impossible or just plain crazy. But right now, as you read these words, somewhere up on one of those peaks a young Englishman is clawing his way into the record books.

At the last count 29-year-old Martin Moran had reached 184 peaks. Winter in the mountaineering calendar last 90 days, starting on December 21 and finishing on March 20, so there are 93 peaks still to be climbed and 35 days in which to do them.

Moran, born on Tyneside, is a chartered accountant who realised his destiny was not to sit in an office keeping somebody else's books. Instead, it was to climb mountains to a height where the cold, glittering across the snow, seems to freeze the air itself.

He has had his wish these past few weeks because the winds on the Scottish summits have been between 60 and 100 miles an hour and the temperature 35 degrees below. You take your glove off to scratch your nose and you have frostbite. And it is easy to lose your hearing, sight and, worst of all, your sense of balance.

"I was on a ridge the other day which should have been easy, but the wind was so fierce I had to crawl. The wind was throwing me about, playing with me." As the man said, mountaineering is a judgment game and sometimes the stakes are life and death.

Club-footed

Most of us would have stayed in the office, content to dream, but not Moran. He and his wife, Joy, a kindred spirit, sold their house to raise the £2500 needed for vehicle hire, petrol, food and equipment. Then they took to the high road. . . .

I met them parked, in snow of course, just north of the Pass of Killiecrankie. That day, despite feeling club-footed from the numbing cold, Moran had reached three peaks in the Grampians and was planning the next day's assault.

Four mountains — An Sgarsoch, Can Ealar, Beinn Dearg and Can a' Clanain—ascents of 5000 feet and 22 miles of walking, much of it, in knee-deep snow, like exploring virgin land.

smoke or eat meat. He is bespectacled and studious-looking. Come to think of it, he looks like an accountant so what the hell is he doing climbing these mountains?

There are two reasons. The first is to raise £50,000 for the charity Intermediate Technology, which works in famine- and poverty-stricken countries. That was the agency, you might recall, for which Richard and Adrian Crane ran 2000 miles along the length of the Himalayas. Moran calls his venture ——mits for Surv——

hoping it will give me a reputation. For instance, anyone who comes to Scotland will say: "Martin Moran must know the Munros like the back of his hand. We'll go to him. It must increase my knowledge as a guide, mustn't it?"

He knows his way up the sides of a mountain, does Moran. He has climbed in the Himalayas and Alaska and conquered the north face of the Eiger. "But I can tell you this winter assault on th——

up, there was a blizzard and we had white-out condition.

"I didn't expect anything to happen but Joy stepped on to a cornice, an edge, of ice. It broke away behind her and I fell off with her. The cornice hit the slope 20 feet below and it avalanched."

There was a low-pitched rumble and suddenly the Morans were sliding, rolling, tumbling down a 200ft slope surrounded by blocks of snow large enough to maim or bury them.

By some miracle, and up there you don't argue about who's pulling the strings, they finished, uninjured, on top of the snow. They had survived what mountaineers describe as a full-depth, wind-slab avalanche 300 yards wide.

As a cynic weaned on professional soccer in which cheating is par for the course, it occurred to me that the Morans could stay in th—— —— van

Mike Herd's feature in the London Evening Standard

and still a further horizon beyond are to be crossed within the next few hours.

Pace yourself, set your watch, divide the daylight hours and ration out the snacks. Then knuckle down and don't stop or you'll lose heart...

> *At 5.30 a final spurt saw me onto Carn Bhac, the eighth Munro, right on the target I'd set on Cairnwell. Fealar Lodge, high on a tributary of the Tilt, was 2 miles to the south-west and would likely provide a barn or at least a wall for shelter. As darkness fell, the haze cleared and a keen frost pinched, so I hurried down towards it. Quite abruptly I was stopped in my tracks at the sight of vehicle headlights flashing nearby. The beams seemed focused directly on my path and I felt a real fear of being hunted. There was no bothy here, no other reason to come. This was surely not a chance encounter! I even switched my own torch off as I cautiously approached the nest of buildings.*

A generator was humming by one of the cottages and in a lighted doorway a bearded figure waited. I had unwittingly arrived at Scotland's highest permanent habitation, and one of its most remote, 500m up and 8 miles from the nearest public road.

Stepping into the light, Jimmy Lean the shepherd looked me up and down until his eyes gleamed in recognition.

'So you'll be the chap who's doing all the Munros this winter', he declared with pinpoint accuracy. Now I know how Doctor Livingstone felt! He ushered me inside where his wife Dorothy already had the kettle boiled for tea. While I gladly drank they engaged me in an hour's non-stop chatter. I was the year's first visitor at Fealar.

'We read you were in the Cairngorms and wondered when you'd come this way', said Dorothy.

Their winter lives are divorced from all normality. On a Monday morning Jimmy takes their daughter down to school at Straloch in the snowcat, and, if conditions allow, will pick her up on Friday but: 'In 1984 she had to stay down for six weeks at lodgings in the big snows.'

Both their sons were working on estates, one down by Atholl, the other over west in Glen Garry. There is no television and a radio telephone is the only outside link, but you could sense their peace, and a contentment in each other's company.

'Winter is a quiet time', he said. 'Just the sheep to feed and a bit of stalking...'

At length he saw my eyelids drooping.

'Well, you'll be needing a bed then...' He took me over to the

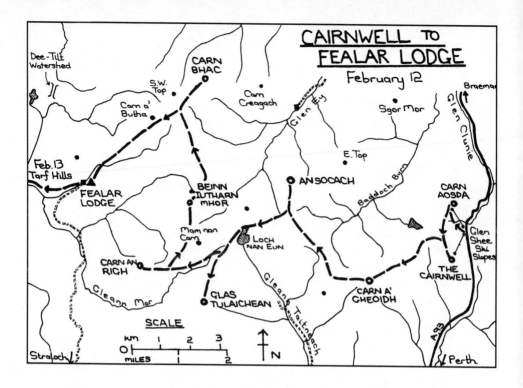

shooting lodge where a choice of six rooms for the night was offered! So instead of curling up in an open sheep pen, I dropped towards slumber stretched out on a double bed, browsing through the back copies of *Country Life,* and feeling quite a distinguished guest.

The two-day wait in Blair Atholl was not an easy time for Joy. Outside, the village life gave a picture of normality which threw a disturbing mirror against her own existence. Suddenly a home and job were missed:

> *I saw the men leave for work, watched housewives go shopping, small children hanging at their skirts, heard the endless idle chatter in the village store — their lives struck me as so mundane at one moment, and at the next I was aching with envy and longing for my own home, and sorely missing that secure job I had gladly abandoned last year. With Martin away, and nothing to do, the point of our venture just vanished from my thoughts…*

Joy had to wait until 7pm for my return. We both felt subdued that night, for the Ring of Tarf and a 7-mile walk out down Glen Tilt had sorely tested my own dedication to the task. In all, the walk from Fealar Lodge was 28 miles, and both terrain and weather were raw accompaniments throughout.

The atmosphere of the snowy Tarf would be hard to match for its sheer intensity. Apart from a walker's bothy in the centre of the Ring, any marks of humanity that do exist are obliterated under the snow. You can be transported back to any era of your choosing and really live out the dream for a few hours. Sound is also absent, for even the wildlife has deserted the moors in winter. Of course the waddling ptarmigan and fleeing grouse are there in plenty, but their cries are harsh and only emphasise the intervening silence. Occasionally a white hare dashes through the tussocks. The deer have sought low grazing, and there are no stampeding herds to stir the spirit. Few of the rarer birds are around, though a flutter of snow buntings may be spotted if you are quick of eye. Even the wandering sheep are missed when absent.

The traveller must plot a skilful route through this country, holding to the hardened snowfields, frozen peat and burnt heather. Today, this meant avoiding the drifted north-west slopes, and pursuing either the exposed crests or icebound streambeds. However, the tougher ground could not be dodged for ever. After a heathery climb up from the Falls of Tarf, An Sgarsoch and Carn Ealar and even the 6-mile valley crossing to the granite crown of Beinn Dearg were firm and fast, but on the western flank of Carn a'Chlamain, my luck ran out:

> The snow looked firm, but just as my balance rocked forward into each new step I would break through the crust and plunge to the knee; so I would aim for the heather but there found only hidden ditches and tangled tussocks which would send me searching back for the snow. As passage was deflected and retarded, the remaining miles grew into an awesome burden.

Anyone who has trekked the Pennine moors under the snows, especially the great bogtrots such as the Derwent Watershed, could echo these sentiments with heartfelt sympathy.

The final plunge into the fault-line trench of the Tilt brought a sudden end to the wilderness. The lower glen is richly ornamented by woodland copses, sweeping drives and pretty cottages, a charming end to any trek however great the fatigue, and even on a dark night.

East of Cairnwell pass the Grampian sprawl bears a further eight Munros before its next major incision at Glen Clova. We drove around to Glen Shee immediately on my return through the portals of the Tilt. The weather was holding its improvement and early morning snow showers only briefly veiled a clear blue sky which at last gave some definition to the distant views.

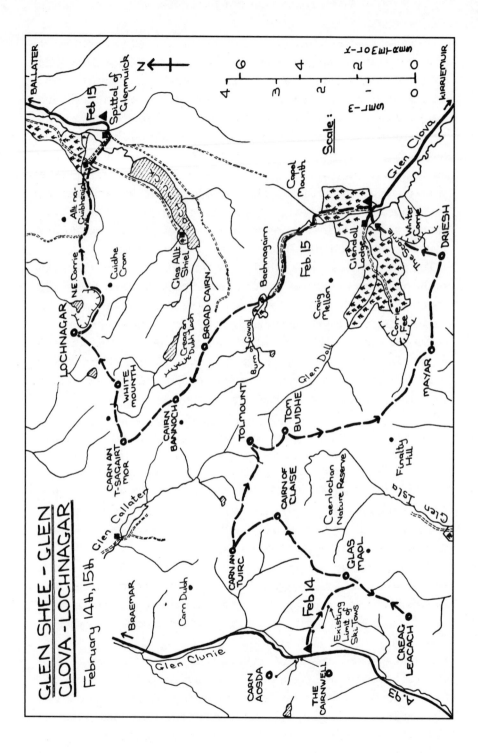

GLEN SHEE – GLEN
CLOVA – LOCHNAGAR
February 14th, 15th

From the head of the ski-tows we detoured south to the walled top of Creag Leacach before traversing the piebald dome of Glas Maol. The top is currently a bone of contention between the skiing and environmental lobbies. An application has been permitted to extend the tows very nearly to the summit to give an appreciable expansion of the Glen Shee ski domain. However, this will encroach on Caenlochan National Nature Reserve, the breeding ground of dotterel and other rare bird species, and seems to breach the Scottish Office Ski Guidelines*. It is unlikely at this stage that the decision will be overturned, but happily the development is subject to several clauses protective to the environment.

For more than fifteen years the capacity of Scotland's downhill ski facilities has been static. Since the plan to extend the Cairn Gorm lifts towards the Lairig Ghru was defeated in 1982 the pressure of increasing demand has become uncontainable. On any fine winter weekend the Scottish resorts are completely overwhelmed, with disgruntled skiers spending the majority of their expensive day waiting in queues. Yet despite this, and for all the fickle weather, they are still prepared to come.

Although Glen Shee has a large untouched potential, it is in the west on Aonach Mor in Lochaber that new development is now imminent. An access road was given planning consent in early 1985 and all parties have pronounced a cautious blessing**. Yet the scenic impact of a wholly new scheme may be severe, and the skier will lack the reliable snow cover that is guaranteed in the east. During the 1984–5 winter season, albeit an exceptional year, the Glencoe slopes were closed for lack of snow for all but three or four weeks. However, Fort William is the undoubted winner, for it desperately needs the new jobs and income which the project promises.

If we were all on Nordic skis the problem would be solved at a stroke. Now there was a bright thought as I trudged away *on foot* towards Tolmount! Yet today the snow was deep enough that I pined for them. Joy had dropped down from Carn an Tuirc to bring the van to Clova.

Mayar and Driesh are Clova's local Munros, and the last of my day. Their shapely summits were a welcome sight during the featureless

---

* The Guidelines state a 'presumption against any significant intrusions into the National Nature Reserves'. In this case the extension is conveniently not being treated as a *significant* intrusion.

** The Aonach Mor ski centre was opened in 1991.

tramp from Tom Buidhe and gave fine glimpses over the scoured edge of the glen. Coire Fee and Driesh's Winter Corrie have good climbing here, especially in the lower grades, and are the local haunts for the denizens of Dundee.

Thirty-two hours on the march out of the last sixty had taken toll of my energy. On the steep descent of The Scorrie my knees collapsed like jellies. I slithered down to level ground then swayed light-headed to the roadend car park. But Joy did not arrive for another hour, harassed by the snowy roads, still depressed from Atholl and suffocated by a head-cold. All the ingredients were there for a blazing row, and I glibly tossed the spark by demurring to fill the water container. The crumpets just requested were promptly hurled rather than served to me, and I was soon outside breaking the ice in the river, my ears still ringing from the retort. After two months cooped like hens it was testimony to our mutual patience that this was our first serious flare-up.

Lochnagar has a greater tradition and romance than any other Scottish mountain, its quality being immortalised in Byron's stirring verse:

> *England! Thy beauties are tame and domestic,*
> *To one who has roved o'er the mountains afar;*
> *Oh for the crags that are wild and majestic!*
> *The steep frowning glories of dark Lochnagar.*

Notwithstanding the summer visitors, the mountain is the true 'monarch' of Balmoral. Its north-eastern corrie is a magnificently proportioned granite bowl, 300m in depth, and after Ben Nevis the country's most famous winter climbing ground. From Glen Clova the route to Lochnagar is indirect, but in its circuit of the Dubh Loch valley achieves the finest high-level traverse in the area, and formed the next link in my Grampian route.

At −11°C the overnight air in the glen had been even more frosty than the atmosphere inside the van! Expecting a repeat of yesterday's drifts I shouldered my skis for the 4-mile approach up the glen's northern fork to Bachnagairn. Here the Burn of Gowal forms a delectable wooded gorge which today was choked with columns of shining ice. Beyond is the featureless climb to the plateau at Broad Cairn.

The Lochnagar massif is geologically twinned with the Cairngorms, being formed of the same igneous intrusion in contrast to the varying schists of the other Grampians. The change of rock is quickly noticed.

Broad Cairn's gentle northern incline breaks with no warning into the Creag an Dubh Loch, a 250m slice of bare pink granite which cuts the flanks for half a mile. The cliff has taken over from Lochnagar in the last two decades as the spearhead of climbing advance in both summer and winter. A look at its compacted overlapping slabs will leave no illusions of the difficulty.

The skis were on and off across the tops, and mainly off on Lochnagar which was blown down to hard ice:

> *This was the first day of calm. Released from the need to fight the cold I relaxed into a drowsy reverie in the sunshine and nearly fell asleep after lunch on Cairn Bannoch!*

From Lochnagar my descent skirted the edge of the great corrie then dropped to Meikle Pap and then Allt-na-giubhsaich. This is the most popular route of approach, revealing the corrie with stunning immediacy and enabling its inspection from below as well as above. The final pitches and exits of Eagle Ridge, the Parallel Gullies, the Black Spout Pinnacle Face and many other great climbs may be identified and admired by the walker sauntering around the rim to the summit tor of Cac Carn Beag.

Glen Muick was soft and tranquil on my arrival, its bottom flats bathed in the warm sunlight of middle afternoon. The square-cut glen is a perfect piece of glacial architecture and with the brooding loch, which spans it from side to side, has a compellingly wild aspect. The Spittal of Glenmuick is merely 7 miles from Clova via the direct Capel Mounth track; but for the driver is a nightmare journey of over 80, and gave Joy one of her most hectic and trying days; witness her diary:

> *I was the first vehicle down Clova, the road a sheet of ice and the ditches waiting open-mouthed to catch a slip of concentration. At Kirriemuir there were two radio interviews to do, and between them a frantic round of shopping. Then to the garage – petrol, oil, water, tyres and propane gas. No gas – so on with the drive and find it en route. The minor road to Glen Shee once again was dangerously drifted. It took three hours to reach Ballater where I arranged to collect Steve Bonnist from the Aberdeen bus, and located our fuel before proceeding up Glen Muick. There was an hour before Martin was due, just time to prepare the van for our guest and make an evening meal. Nothing had touched my lips since 7am!*

Beyond Lochnagar the Grampians slowly lose their momentum and only at Mount Keen is the 3,000ft contour again attained. But although it is the most easterly Munro, there are a further 30 miles of moor and glen before the Aberdeenshire coast is met. The hill is most easily ascended from Glen Esk to its south, from which an old mounth road crosses close to the top. By comparison, the way from Glen Muick over Cairn Hillock has a long stretch of peatland to cross before the final cone, which is a painful plod in deep snow. Though only a 12-mile return distance this was not for me the respite desired before our return to the Cairngorms. But the weather was superlative, the burning sun making us glad of cream and glasses. Yet every patch of shade was like a three-star freezer. A whole week of sub-zero temperatures had now elapsed, so still the snowdrifts lay unbonded.

We were joined by Steve, who was in Scotland to make arrangements for the coming climax of the journey. At a total of 198 Munros, the finish was not *so* far away. But as we sat at lunch just beneath the summit all complacency was shattered by the arrival of two hardy-looking walkers on the top. One of them thumped the summit trig point and exclaimed: 'Ah ha, just one more to go!'

So at last we were to meet him! The anonymous competitor, whom I had often imagined secretly at work these last two months, always sneaking on a step ahead, was now ready to take the winter Munros glory, and render my own venture a nonsense. Bonnist blanched; all his charitable efforts were about to crumble. Our curiosity soon became unbearable. I ambled over as though to pass the time of day...

'Doing the Munros are you?'

'Aye, and only Ben Lomond left', came the triumphant reply.

'Taken long then?' I must have been visibly twitching in anticipation, but his bearded countenance broke into a roar of laughter.

'Oh, the better part of twenty years, I'm afraid to say!'

However entertaining, the episode later raised a more serious reflection:

Why the fear of being upstaged? What if he had said 'two months'? I might have cursed and brooded for a day or so, but would I ever think of giving up? Of course not, and all power to him if he had done it! The prime motivation for me must be personal challenge. The lure to be first is only a secondary spur, and though undeniably a strong incentive, I hope it will never be my lord and master.

Even taken in isolation, the last hard days had brought great fulfilment, for a solo crossing of the Grampians is a test of will, and a lasting restorative for the mind.

12

THE CAIRNGORMS COMPLETE

17–21 February:
Beinn Bhrotain – Braeriach – Ben Macdui – Ben Avon –
Cairn Gorm

The River Dee has the pre-eminent claim on the drainage of the high Cairngorms. The trickles of the melting snows give its birth 1,250m up on the Braeriach plateau. This tiny sub-Arctic stream plunges down and through the greatest corrie of the massif, then gathers the tributary waters of the Derry, Luibeg and Quoich to its girth, and broadens into graceful maturity through the Forests of Mar and Balmoral. Comparing the claims of the other major rivers, the Spey all but ignores the range apart from the collection of the Feshie, whilst the Avon seems so embarrassed by its capture of Macdui's waters that it rushes out of the mountains without a pause. Deeside therefore undoubtedly forms the most natural and grandest route of entry, which has long been a pilgrimage to all who seek the lonely plateaux.

Already repelled in our attempt from the north, it was now imperative to gain a foothold on the range by this southern approach, even though it meant stretching my endurance to the limit on each clear day that followed. The non-stop Grampian traverse had only just regained the ground lost in the windstorm. Now there was a chance to capitalise on that effort. A three-day round from the Linn of Dee roadhead could encompass all the fifteen outstanding Munros of the massif given a continuation of the excellent conditions. We chose to start from the west with Braeriach, Cairn Toul and their subsidiaries, and packed our sacks late into the night.

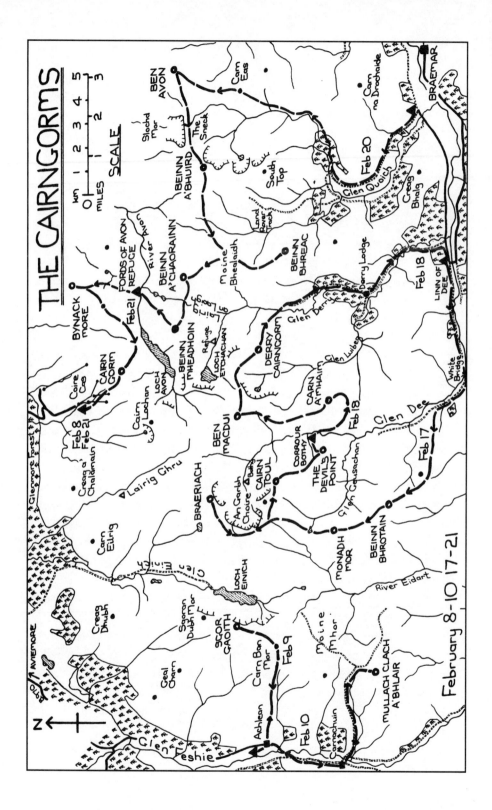

THE CAIRNGORMS

SCALE

km 0 1 2 3 4 5

miles 0 1 2 3

N

February 8-10 17-21

The twilight temperature of −13°C sent us off towards White Bridge at a swinging quickmarch. Its sudden stimulus was much required, for we had risen in a soporific stupor, due partly to fatigue but mainly as a result of my mistakenly setting our alarm for 4.30 instead of 5.30. Mornings were tough enough already without such catastrophe, but an early start would no doubt pay us back by sunset.

The Cairngorms are the 'blue hills', although they are actually composed of red granite. However, the tundra landscape of the high tops does have a distinctly bluish wash when viewed at a distance, in refreshing contrast to the brown heather moors of the nearby Grampians. The effect is especially pronounced in winter when the snow's refraction adds an icy tingle to the hue, and it inspired a growing vigour to our ascent of the patchwork slopes towards Beinn Bhrotain that was climaxed by the rise of the sun over Lochnagar. Streams of cloud idled at the higher levels and threw our silhouettes into foggy shadows and ghostly spectres, but the summit pierced these mists into an azure sky, against which the white sweep of the highest plateaux made a brilliant relief.

Bhrotain and Monadh Mor led us around the skyline of Glen Geusachan and onto the featureless back of Cairn Toul. Lunch was taken at Loch nan Stuirteag before the climb. Again, no wind disturbed our rest, but the sun had faded above a coverlet of cloud which infiltrated from the west. The Tarf and Feshie hills were close in view. Mullach Clach a'Bhlair was but a dull and dingy bump on the Great Moss, hardly seeming the scene for our 'Alaskan' battle just a week ago.

After a tiresome plod the crest was gained near Einich Cairn, where An Garbh Choire makes its deepest bite into the plateau. This is the Cairngorms' greatest amphitheatre, a mile and a half in width and with a nest of hanging corries etching its 4-mile rim. As recently as 1810 the coire may have held a small glacier, a suggestion based on the dating of lichen on its terminal moraines, and there are still permanent snowfields through most years. Though we are now in a phase of climatic warming, it would take only a slight reversal to bring the Ice Age back to the Cairngorms.*

---

* Gordon Manley has estimated that a 2°C drop in average annual temperature, if sustained for fifteen years, would be sufficient to re-establish permanent moving icefields in the high corries, though there is minimal likelihood of this happening in the short-term future.

In direct contravention of the climbing rules we left our sacks on the edge to make the long detour to Braeriach. It is a dubious tactic and should be entertained only in settled visibility, but on countless occasions through the winter it saved me vital time and strength. The Braeriach-Cairn Toul circuit is the most exhilarating plateau walk in the Cairngorms. In winter it is part of the 4,000ft tops ski-tour which gives a hard but magnificent day's expedition from Glen More, and is usually feasible for many weeks of a normal winter owing to its high elevation. But though the cover on the tops was now complete, the surface was icy and with the snow-base as high as 600m the skis would have been more a hindrance than a help.

Joy found the head of An Garbh Choire an intimidating spot:

> *The cornices hung over the edges like huge jaws ready to snap; their sight enough to make me shudder. As the cloud spread and the light flattened I became more than a little anxious to get back to the sacks and off the plateau...*

She might, however, have taken a leaf out of Richard McHardy's book of tricks. A few years ago he applied his inimitable panache to demonstrate how the cornices can be tamed to one's advantage. On a filthy day when Richard considered the snow conditions too dangerous to join his mates on a climbing route on the corrie walls, he ambled alone up an easy gully onto The Angel's Peak and over the plateau. Trying to find his way back in the mist he walked straight onto a snow edge which collapsed and carried him down for over 300m, stopping conveniently near the Garbh Choire Bothy door. Up he stepped, miraculously unhurt, and wandered in for an early tea, quite unruffled by a plunge which made our avalanche on Wyvis look like child's play. Such style must take many years of practice!

The summit wedge of Cairn Toul in both its shape and perched position is the finest top in the Cairngorms, but we hurried on, for it was the next and last Munro of the day which held a special significance for Joy; but:

> *With the abundance of beautiful Gaelic names for the Scottish peaks why should I get landed with 'The Devil's Point' for my 100th summit of the season!*

From the Point it was an initially steep but fast descent to Corrour Bothy. How welcoming it is when your night's refuge lies directly beneath, fully in view and is a simple descent in the last daylight. Corrour had a few other visitors as is usual, for it is a popular staging post on the Lairig Ghru route, but we squeezed in and were laid out on the floor by 8pm, the prospect of a glorious ten-hour sleep banishing all concerns of cornices and approaching blizzards.

Answering Nature's call half-way through the night, my torchbeam struck a myriad of floating flakes and a barrier of white fog outside. I hurried back to my warm cocoon of sleep and dreams but later, as the milky light of dawn filtered through the bothy windows, reality had to be confronted. To be trapped in a bothy by a blizzard was the most disastrous scenario that could be envisaged for us, but now we had to face the situation and juggle the options:

Plan A: stay put and stretch supplies for the extra day that would now be required to get over Ben Avon – hungry and very boring.

Plan B: retreat to the van; 6 miles down, a comfortable rest, then 6 miles back with more supplies when the storm cleared – 12 miles of extra effort and still a day lost.

Plan C: go on over Macdui's four Munros, leaving Cairn Gorm for a separate day; stop at the Hutchison Hut in Coire Etchachan tonight and hope to do Ben Avon tomorrow – if it improves.

A and B were safe but woefully depressing. C was the daring option but rather risky. However, since there was no perceptible wind at the bothy and as the Macdui tops were all familiar to me, it quickly gained my preference. But Joy was set against Plan C from the moment of its inception, and immediately withdrew. Having inspected the map of Macdui in great detail she was already well acquainted with the Coire Sputan Dearg, the Loch Etchachan cliffs, and the Loch Avon basin, and there was not a hope of tempting her anywhere within five miles of their edges in a white-out, whatever my claims to navigational skill!

Now realising that the next two days would be spent in solitude with only a compass needle for comfort, my own resolve was lost. The decision had been reached on hard-baked rationality and bound me fast, but underneath it I was all along banking on Joy's company. Our parting on the crest of the Luibeg path was therefore charged with such emotion that anyone would have thought I was setting off for the North Pole. Joy hated seeing me embark on an exploit that she herself declared unsafe:

In the dense mist we rearranged the loads, Martin standing like an iceberg, his solemn face no doubt hiding only bitterness at my letting him down. As he walked off towards Carn a'Mhaim, my tears began to flow and I cried despairingly 'take care!' A faint 'aye aye' floated back but he was already swallowed up by the cloud and beyond recall.

Joy, however, was unaware that this steely exterior was only a front to my own anguish. Had my true emotions escaped, Macdui would have been missed, and doubtless regretted later. But for the first time in sixty days my enthusiasm for the tops ran completely dry:

With no heart for the task, every step of the ascent was a torture. I ate my lunch long before a mid-morning snack was due, but this only left me more in want of succour. And frequent rests simply put me further behind the cursed clock! I passed into the throes of yawning depression for a good two hours before accepting my rotten lot.

The top of Scotland's second highest mountain is a gentle and feature-less dome. My navigation proceeded first on directional bearing and then by gauging distance travelled. From the head of the Tailor's Burn to the summit is 750m at 300 degrees, which converts to 450 of my double paces. Counting sheep may induce sleep, but not so counting steps in a white-out. When the total is reached and no trace of the top is visible, then comes the time to worry; but it is preferable to have a vain confidence which says, 'Perhaps they've moved the cairn' rather than dissolving into a 'Help, I'm lost!' panic. A block search of each surrounding hundred metre square eventually brought success. Absolute self-belief is one's only ally in the search.

Sitting beside the crowning tumulus my sympathies went out to the aspirant mountain guides who were that week undergoing their winter climbing assessment at Glenmore Lodge, for no doubt today would have been chosen for their navigation test. Suddenly I realised that not so far away there were other tormented souls even less fortunate than myself, for I vow that a month of isolation would be preferable to a foggy day finding spot heights on the Cairn Lochan plateau, with a Lodge examiner breathing down your neck.

During my own test in 1984, Choe Brookes and I had suffered near disaster. Inevitably, white-out conditions prevailed and on this day a bitter 60mph wind added to the pleasures:

'OK, Martin, you do the next leg – take me to that ring contour south of Coire Domhain,' ordered the grim-faced Bob Barton who has been the scourge of a generation of hapless candidates. As I prepared my bearing, a sudden gust of wind tore the plastic-coated map out of my hands, and flapping like a concertina it disappeared into the cloud. I received a long frost-caked stare from Bob that could only spell 'FAIL'!

'Over to you then, Choe,' he said. I felt like jumping over the nearest cornice at that particular instant.

But just as Choe unfolded his own map, another blast of wind swept across (does the Lodge have a divine hand in these matters?) and though he fumbled gamely, it too was plucked from his grasp. Long silent seconds and then the *coup de grâce*:

'Well, perhaps we could borrow *your* map please, Bob?' I was polite but obviously desperate, but an emphatic 'No!' was the reply.

Meanwhile Choe saved our bacon by digging out a tatty old one-inch sheet, fortuitously brought along as a spare, from the bottom of his sack. Clinging to it for dear life we got Bob off the plateau and escaped with only a severe censure.

Yet we should be glad of the rigorous standards of mountain training which Glenmore Lodge has set over the past twenty-five years, whether we be guides, instructors, teachers or youth leaders. In the five years between 1979 and 1983 there were only 29 serious rescue incidents and 12 fatalities in the Cairngorms and Grampians in winter – no cause for complacency, but viewed against the rapid increases in the numbers of hill-goers, a remarkably low frequency of occurrence[*]. That the current level of accidents in winter is no greater is in large part due to the Lodge's work.

And now my own training was applied in full measure to traverse round the head of Coire Sputan Dearg and onto Derry Cairngorm, all the way in white blindness:

> Already it was 3pm. Beinn Mheadhoin, the fourth Munro, would take at least one and a half hours and leave very little light for finding the hut. A wind was rising fast and a blizzard looked to be in the offing. In fact all the makings of a major epic were gathering together. And then came the thought that tomorrow was a momentous occasion – my thirtieth birthday – and would undoubtedly be better spent in rest and celebration with Joy at Braemar than shivering in a stormbound 'howff' sans food or fuel.

[*] However, the annual numbers of incidents for the whole of Scotland rose from 60 in 1974 to 157 in 1984 and to 339 in 1995. Full accident statistics are published annually in the SMC Journal.

The extra 5 miles of a retreat by Glen Derry were brushed aside by my overwhelming urge to get down. Nor was any disgrace felt after having valiantly forced myself over three Munros; so the earlier agonies were superseded by a carefree homewards romp.

My descent dropped steeply down the eastern flanks. In the upper Derry straggling survivors of the native pine forests bent and groaned in the wind, which whistled unchallenged through the glen. The trees seemed to be withering under the storm's assault, shrinking back to leave a snowy desert in the higher reach. Only down by Derry Lodge does the forest thicken sufficiently to give warmth and security; and at dusk was filled with sheltering herds of deer. The return walk raised my total mileage for the past week to 140. No wonder my knees were wincing on the final stretch of icy track. But what a surprise there was in store for Joy:

> *Having heard the snow and gale warnings on the 6pm forecast, I was settling down for an evening alone feeling very morose and sorrowing for my desertion this morning. Then I heard footsteps crunching up to the back door which thankfully was locked just in case of intruders; but unbelievably it was Martin's voice which called out. I opened it and there he stood grinning broadly: 'Thought I'd come back for my birthday!' he announced and jumped up in.*

The names of Ben Avon and Beinn a'Bhuird are synonymous with long hard days in the hills. Even by the exacting standards of the other Cairngorms these eastern tops are depressingly remote. The ascent of both main Munros in a single day demands a dour determination, winter or summer, but is nought compared to the crossing of all their subsidiary tops, which on Ben Avon alone involves a journey of $6^1/_2$ miles all above the 3,000ft level. Not surprisingly, the four great corries of Beinn a'Bhuird have lagged behind Lochnagar and the Loch Avon cirque in their winter development though they yield little in quality to either. A productive visit here requires at least one overnight bivouac or camp beneath the cliffs.

The storm had proved neither severe nor prolonged, but was enough to make me glad to be off the hill. It left a couple of inches of fresh snow on the tops and gave a day of drizzle as we rested down at Braemar, but over the next night the stars were reborn, and all was set for my final bid. To see the Cairngorms complete at last would be a sweet success.

Glen Quoich provides the shortest access to Ben Avon, yet it is still

10 miles from the road at Linn of Quoich to the summit. The upper part of the glen, where the water meanders between sandy banks under a canopy of Scots Pines, is of exquisite beauty. Yet it had a forlorn atmosphere, for the widely-spaced stands with their stunted growths and fallen branches give a strong breath of decay. Slow climatic change is largely responsible. Warming weather and most especially increased rainfall have caused a progressive acidification of the soils, and while the peat moors burgeoned the trees have died off. However, the over-grazing of deer has greatly accelerated the process in the last two centuries. Only by fencing the remaining areas to keep the deer off the new seedlings, and by expensive ploughing to drain the ground, could the spiral of decline now be reversed. It was these great old forests that first inspired my own love for the Cairngorms, and many a long mile can pass unnoticed in the enchantment of their company.

Joy came with me to the final trees. Looking up at the beckoning tops as they glowed pink with the sunrise, she was understandably envious of my striding off towards them, but was spared a tough 2 miles breaking trail in the fresh drifts of the open valley.

The new snow gave me some misgivings, for there was a long day ahead; but the tops were once again coated by a solid crust of ice to give a perfect walking surface. Bhuird's array of corries captured all my attention on the long pull over Carn Eas, and conditions must have also been good for ice-climbing judging from the opaque smears and streaks in their major clefts and gullies.

Ben Avon's summit is a striking granite tor some 15m in height, a fine example of the many such 'warts' which outcrop on the eastern plateaux. Their formation has long been a mystery, but by latest opinion they are dated to a pre-glacial period when the region experienced a sub-tropical climate and deep weathering under the soil mantle attacked the granite joint-lines. The embryonic features were then exhumed during glaciation, and have survived only on the plateaux tops which were spared erosive destruction under the ice.

The Sneck saddle provides a neat connection from Avon to Beinn a'Bhuird. The trough of Slochd Mor and the Mitre Ridge of the Garbh Choire are excitingly positioned on its northern side, but the scenery deteriorates profoundly on the dull eastern side of the mountain. A Land-Rover track has been driven to a height of 1,100m on this flank to assist in deer stalking and occasionally provide vehicular access for spring skiing.

The gentle slopes of the Cairngorms are particularly vulnerable to disfigurement by bulldozed roads. Only since 1980 have landowners been required to obtain planning permission to drive new tracks above the 300m level, and then only in the specified 'National Scenic Areas'. Yet it is clear that these procedures have been little heeded. Whilst many new roads have appeared, only a handful of planning applications have ever come before the Countryside Commission*. Not only are these tracks insensitively routed, but most are improperly drained and will likely trigger severe future erosion, while their economic necessity has never been properly demonstrated by the owners.

At least the ski developments visibly benefit a huge number of users. However, it is unlikely that a lift system will ever be constructed on these remote eastern tops, and long may their snows remain the domain of the ski mountaineer. Linking Ben Avon and Beinn a'Bhuird to the four-thousanders creates probably the ultimate quest to the long-distance tourer, the traverse of the 'Six Tops'. A one-day crossing was first made in 1962 by Adam Watson, and more recently was done in a round trip from Derry Gate by Raymond Simpson and Rob Ferguson in 1983 in nineteen hours of skiing with five hours' sleep at Corrour Bothy.

A broad moss, the Moine Bhealaidh, separates Beinn a'Bhuird from the central Cairngorms, and rises to a Munro at each end of its 3-mile stretch. These two, Beinn Bhreac and Beinn a'Chaorainn completed my scheduled route, but to their west on the far side of the Lairig an Laoigh, Beinn Mheadhoin was still outstanding from the curtailed Macdui round. Though it increased the day's mileage to 27 and ascent to 1,920m (6,300ft), the 400m climb out of the Lairig felt effortless. My day off had created ample new reserves of stamina to call upon, and so I won the race to reach the summit tor before the sun was lost. The Cuillin apart, this was technically the most difficult top of the winter, only 12m but at least grade II under a half-inch coat of verglas. The sunset, however, moved me to a rapturous diary entry that night down in the Fords of Avon howff:

> Shifting mists had draped themselves across the high plateaux, through which Mheadhoin's summit stacks protruded, and were fired to the deepest bronze. The glory of the Cairngorms was at its apogee this evening.

---

* Now reorganised as Scottish Natural Heritage.

my toes absolutely still on the slippy holds, and yet I was quickly absorbed by the task. The climbing was a craft in itself, a progress of stealth not strength, and slowly the Pinnacle yielded, the arête leaning back until we found ourselves crawling the last few feet to the top block. Without ado we fixed the rope and abseiled off, while Alan filmed the sequence through the milky cloud.

The moment of reaching safety after a long and perilous journey is surely the sweetest that the climber knows. Touching *terra firma* from the abseil brought to us that joyous release from tension. How wonderful it felt to amble back to the glen, hands in pockets. Though the Cuillin were still only half complete there was a brief chance to relax and celebrate the measure of success that we had extracted from the day. And to think that last week had seen me bitterly bemoaning the absence of winter. Well, Skye had given the sharpest retort!

Blaven (Bla Bheinn) is the Island's twelfth Munro, isolated from the Cuillin Ridge, but part of the same igneous intrusion that slowly cooled into the coarse gabbro rock which so delights the summer climber. In common with its neighbours, the mountain's flanks are seamed with gully clefts, and break into some fine cliffs. The only easy side is to the south-east where a track ascends from Loch Slapin into Coire Uaigneich above which the summit is a dispiriting 500m slog on screes.

It formed a suitable interval to the Main Ridge performance, for next day produced the expected gale and an icy rain. Once in control of the weather the westerly depressions are hard to unseat. Both Andy and Alan Thomson had returned to work commitments, and Alan Hinkes was now my sole partner. The snow that so dominated yesterday's events had almost disappeared. We were assisted up the final slopes by a strange updraught. This was but a small eddy from the blasting tempest that was met on top. Quickly chilled to the bone by driving sleet we tried to hurry down, but soon lost our route. How then do you pick the correct line out of a parallel row of identical gullies, some of which ended in hanging chockstones and vertical chimneys? Twice we climbed back up before locating a run of pounded scree that led to safety.

So the northern six were left to do, effectively the only real barrier to my final success. None of the other twenty Munros posed any comparable difficulty, and there were days aplenty to ride out a serious storm.

With claws sharpened we waited for the weather's signal, and it came on cue at dawn the next day. Just as before the Affric trip, the wind magically subsided, and the mists were fast dispersing when we rejoined the Ridge at 9am on Sgurr na Banachdich. However, the cooling air of a cold front passage had chased the dying rain and dropped a coat of verglas on the tops in the last hours of the storm; so crampons were essential wear until the day warmed up. The climbing was intricate in the icy parts, but never treacherous in the manner of two days ago. By keeping my head and a steady pace the horn of Gillean would eventually come, and in Alan I had a climber of implacable enthusiasm as well as an inveterate talker to help me there. Each twist and surprise in the route was relished, and there was even time to look about and admire the Cuillin country...

The central portion of the Ridge is the least known, and the most complex topographically, so whilst the technical difficulties do not match those of the famous obstacles, it is here that many climbers will find themselves in doubt of the route, perplexed by mist, and at the nearest to abandoning their attempt. This is also the section where winter parties must make their bivouac, and the many walled shelters on the level terraces and cols bear witness to their trials. Patey and party were royally accommodated on Banachdich, having had a cache of food and equipment left in place, while Cathcart on his unsupported solo had a miserable night at An Dorus with a 'howling wind driving spindrift across the ridge'.

Open bivouacs can variously be exalting or murderous but either way are the most intense of mountain experiences, whether you are entertained by shooting stars and a moonlight sonata, or else sitting soaked to the skin and praying for the dawn that never seems to come. It was a disappointment of this expedition that I was denied the opportunity, but the bothies were simply too numerous and convenient to be overlooked. The Cuillin Ridge apart, bivouacs in the Highlands are usually contrived by choice or enforced by weather, but rarely the sole expedient.

The trio of summits, Banachdich, Ghreadaidh and Mhadaidh are closely linked, but beyond the latter is a long and kinking route to gain the next Munro at Bruach na Frithe. The ridge first swings east over three pinnacled subsidiary tops, then turns north at Bidein Druim nan Ramh which itself has three summits, all deeply incised by basalt dyke lines. On the Bidein at least one abseil is needed in full winter conditions, and Cathcart nearly came to grief here when his rope dislodged from a poor spike. He slid on steep snow for 15m before the line luckily snagged on a flake and brought him to a halt.

Arrival at Bruach na Frithe brings one onto home ground. Gillean has been bobbing on the horizon throughout the central crocodile, but at last has fixed its place and is immediately accessible beyond the Bhasteir Tooth. Andy Hyslop had taken just twenty-six minutes from here to the finish of his record run, despite suffering from a lack of liquid and glucose, for he had not eaten since the Pinnacle. Compare the torments of Beatty and Beighton on their north–south winter traverse in 1978. They had taken three hours simply in effecting the abseil off the Tooth when their ropes jammed hopelessly.

No such problems were presented to Alan and myself. Naismith's Route on the Tooth was only a little damp and lichenous, the morning ice having long ago melted in a weak sun, returning us to summer conditions. Though well furnished with jugs and cracks it is never-theless a remarkably steep and exposed pitch considering that its inauguration date was 1896.

Am Basteir, its Munro parent, lies just beyond, and then only a 'Moderate' chimney bars the ridge to Gillean. We were soon perched on its airy top and enjoying a vast prospect over the tablelands of the northern island which for once glowed soft and warm.

Again we could enjoy a late afternoon descent from the black peaks in leisured satisfaction. A fine day on Skye is as rare in its quality as it is in occurrence, a jewel to be coveted for long months after. As we dropped by the Bhasteir gorge and out onto the moors towards Sligachan there wasn't even a single midge to disturb the pleasure. Whatever the adventures encountered on the Ridge a winter trip to the Cuillin is worth trying for that joy alone!

Alan dined heartily and then departed on his journey back to Newcastle*. Later I rang Steve Bonnist and proudly reported that success within the ninety days was almost assured. But suddenly this was not enough:

'We need a definite finishing date, Martin. I've got a battery of jour-nalists and television crews ready to come to Fort William but they

---

* After 1985 Alan Hinkes achieved tremendous success on the 8,000m peaks of the Himalaya, climbing eight of them, including Everest and K2. In 1997 he was planning further trips to climb the remaining six 8,000ers and thus become the first British climber to complete all fourteen. Maybe then he will finish the Munros!

need three days' notice, and we must tell *Blue Peter* when you'll be coming… '

I instantly totted up the score… three days at Achnashellach, two days to the Ben, and one day spare for a storm…

'Make it the thirteenth then', I replied. That would be an eighty-three days' total, not bad even considering the luck with the weather…

But how can wild mountains be subjected to the beck and command of the media? Could they be so shackled, they wouldn't be 'mountains' as such, and I certainly would have had little interest in climbing them for the last eleven weeks. Driving out of Skye with a full moonbeam lighting the waters of the Inner Sound I was struck by the sudden impulse that I must go out again that night and onto the Achnashellach peaks. Instinct was telling me something, yet with my bed so close at hand and in the sleepy wake of a filling meal, the message was ignored and slowly slipped from view.

15

THE FINAL SURGE

8–13 March:
Achnashellach – Loch Monar hills – Ben Nevis and
the Grey Corries

There was no second chance to beat the storm. By 8am the rain was drumming its merry tune on the roof of the van, and the trees at Achnashellach were swaying in time to the gathering wind. Opportunity knocks but once, though exactly when in the night the front arrived cannot be said, for my blissful dreams were undisturbed.

The mountain ranges on either side of Glen Carron filled the last blanks on the Western Highlands map. The glen is a major junction between massive and rounded schistose hills to the south, and the exciting laminations of the Torridonian peaks. On this north side are three Munros, which join with three lower but equally fine summits, Fuar Tholl, An Ruadh-stac and Beinn Damh, to bridge the gap to Glen Torridon itself. All of it is deer forest, a bright and open land of quartz-capped tops and a sprinkling of lochans...

But not today. The sky was laden with moisture, and only after prolonged deliberation did we set out at all, winding up the stalker's track and into Coire Lair. At a height of 400m, Beinn Liath Mhor was already half won, but a booming wind rocked us in our steps and forced a crucial pause. Flurries of white wavelets blew across the corrie lochan, and the encircling peaks frowned as black as thunder. And then a squalling rain joined with the gale to drive away altogether my fading resolution:

No doubt the hills could have been climbed, albeit with a struggle, but
though I probed the recesses of my mind, not an ounce of will was there to
draw from. With a heavy heart but no delay I called to Joy that I'd had
enough.

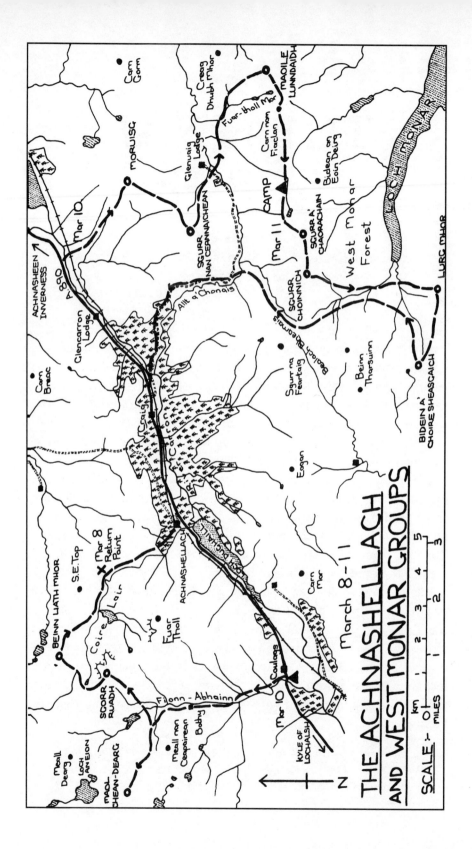

THE ACHNASHELLACH
AND WEST MONAR GROUPS

March 8-11

SCALE :-

km 0 1 2 3 4 5

MILES 1 2 3

Plodding back down, I roundly cursed last night's surrender to crea-
ture comforts. The moonlight scheme had sounded crazy but it was a
flash of intuition which had a chance of success. My want of response
marked a symbolic retreat from the fight. And now of course a timely
storm had come along to open up the crack, and found me defenceless.
All day the tempest clamoured its victory, giving no real hope of a
repeal, while with every passing hour, March 13 pressed down its
claim:

> We mused away the afternoon both feeling 'prisoners' of our own making.
> Until the Munros are finished our lives hang suspended. Our desire for a
> long unpressured rest, our search for a home, my guiding career up here in
> the Highlands, nothing can progress. Just five more days of storm and yet I
> cannot face them.

The following day saw me lowered deeper into the trap. The weather
remained foul from dawn to dusk, yet bore the same agonising possibility that I could have gone out had I possessed the courage. Rain,
strong wind and cloud are an unpleasant mix, but pose no immediate
threat to survival, and so another day was squandered.

Every radio forecast was optimistic for a clearance, but the front was
loath to pass away and stayed firmly entrenched over the north-west
margins. The remainder of Scotland lay under a stable ridge of colder
air, but there was nowhere else for us to escape to, as had been so easy
earlier in the winter. The long hours of daylight gave ample time for
introspection:

> There is not a glimmer of inspiration in these warm westerly storms, and
> I've shut off my mind to them, yet underneath I'm clinging to the blithe
> reliance that they will pass away. To be on Ben Nevis by 10am on the 13th
> as promised, will demand an enormous effort even in fine conditions...

For apart from the three Munros to our north there were seven to the
south of Achnashellach, which included the sequestered peaks of the
West Monar Forest, Lurg Mhor and Bidein a'Choire Sheasgaich. This
pair rival Seana Bhraigh and A'Mhaighdean in the romantic lure of
inaccessibility, and the district has no nearby shieling or bothy for an
overnight stop. All these ten now had to be squeezed into the following
two days and, without a pause, the greater part of the Grey Corries plus
the last two Mamores completed on the third. A total of 20 Munros, 62
miles and *30,000ft* of ascent was proposed in three and a quarter days.

Joy was powerless to help me through the barrier:

> *On every brightening in the clouds I would make a cheerful report in the*
> *hope that Martin might be jolted into action; but underneath I was*
> *somehow confident that he would recover by his own devices and make the*
> *final surge. From long experience I knew that he works best when under*
> *pressure...*

The rain came in heavier bursts in the evening, yet with thick-skinned optimism we sat in the van drafting and typing the post-expedition reports: 'I can honestly say your equipment contributed significantly to my *success...*' and other fraudulent presumptions. Bedtime was 8.30, with a play on the radio and still the rat-tat-tat of the rain on the window an inch from my nose.

Four o'clock, and a brief stirring to hear again the familiar sound of the drizzle. At 5am the alarm rings out, crisis point is reached; there can be no turning over and no more excuses. A peep through the curtain shows a shy moon filtering through the cloud, and the wind no longer bellows. Luck is back with us; up like a shot, on with the kit, and out by 6am, Joy striding ahead up the stony path from Coulags:

> *The first 2 miles were murderous. Splashing through pools, sinking in the*
> *peat, and tripping in the hidden ruts up to the disused bothy by the*
> *Fionnabhainn. The huge effort ahead was painful to contemplate; but then*
> *a bright dawn emerged and we left the valley marsh for the white rock*
> *ramparts of Maol Chean-dearg. Without consciously trying my muscles*
> *started to fire and my torpor lifted. The 'show' was back on the road...*

The Torridonian three were being taken in reverse sequence from our first attempt in the hope of relieving the initial anguish of setting out, so my morning's route would finish down Coire Lair. Maol Cheandearg is ringed by a superb stalking path at half-height, from which its summit cone rises as a jumbled mass of quartzite boulders. The top still lay in mist on our arrival.

Joy's standard-bearing role was now fulfilled, and having reversed the ascent she watched me leap precariously across the swollen burn and romp up onto the 750m western flank of Sgorr Ruadh, happily confident that no further encouragement was required. Then it was a quick trot back to Coulags to make ready for our next stage.

Both Sgorr Ruadh and Fuar Tholl have impressive faces to the Lair basin on their north-east sides. Fuar Tholl's Mainreachan Buttress is considered one of the finest sandstone precipices in the country, while Ruadh's more broken cliffs have several winter gullies and ridges. The latter were first explored by the Reverend Robertson in 1898. In contrast, their south-west slopes are a featureless unbroken sweep. This is the rule with the majority of our mountains. Over 90 per cent of Scotland's glacial corries lie in the quadrant between north and east, which reflects the prevalence of the south-westerly airstream throughout the Ice Ages. This caused maximum accumulation of snow and therefore the concentration of glaciers on the lee sides of the hills.

The airy edge of Sgorr Ruadh was an exciting completion to a gruelling climb. The summit was frosted by a brisk wind which sent the cloud balls scudding across from the north-west both above and between the mountain tops. Beinn Liath Mhor was gained by swinging north around the valley head, and then a steep and stony drop brought me back to the corrie floor and the place of our retreat two days ago. The direct descents on this south-western side of the mountain are fraught with outcrops and scree shoots, and especially in snow conditions are to be discouraged in favour of the longer traverse over the south-east tops.

Joy had worked marvellously to have hot soup and lunch waiting, as well as our camping sack packed, by my arrival at Achnashellach at 11.50. She had also reaffirmed to Intermediate Technology that the thirteenth was still our target. Now there was confidence for you; but the signs were promising. Today had mellowed into a settled sunshine, and my spirit was so vibrant that leaving the van after a thirty-minute break felt no great hardship.

From a dropping point 4 miles up the road past Glencarron Lodge, my steps hastened onto Moruisg, the nearest of the Munros on the southern side. Unknowingly, the two last despairing days had served to replenish my energy. Moruisg, its neighbour, Sgurr nan Ceannaichean, and the descent to Glenuaig Lodge took little over two hours. Joy did not arrive for another ten minutes, having parked at Craig and shouldered a 40lb pack for the 6-mile trek up the Allt a'Chonais glen.

After a quick conference to fix our campsite for that night we parted again, myself springing off towards Maoile Lunndaidh while Joy lugged the load to a height of 600m in the north-east valley of Sgurr a'Chaorachain. My last mountain of the day was also the bulkiest, and its broad summit plateau was sheathed in ice and fringed by corniced corries of which the Fuar-tholl Mor looked particularly impressive. Winter was still fully in control here, an extra 100m in altitude and a further 5 miles inland creating a surprising change in the conditions, and making me glad of having axe and crampons.

The softening of the scenery from the Torridon district was reassuring. Rolling along the southern horizon beyond Loch Monar were the Affric and Cannich hills – already a month in the memory. Indeed, in every direction of the spacious view the mountains were familiar, most of them firm friends, but a few like Wyvis still repellent. Truly the ring was closing and the end was near.

From the shivering top of Maoile Lunndaidh my eyes dropped to the silent shelter of the corrie, and could just pick out Joy's red jacket moving to and fro about our tiny green tent, which was sited on a curve in the burn. If not a bivouac, then at least the winter was granting me one high camp.

> *Tea was nearly boiled, and quickly feeling the chill of my perspiration, I dived inside to warmth and rest. Propped on our elbows, weary legs glowing in their sleeping bags, and our hearts pulsing as one, we have watched the evening colours fade and the stars light up in the darkening sky; what a perfect haven!*
>
> *There is still much to do, but the biggest day is off my chest; only six Munros, but 3,570m (11,700ft) of ascent and 23 miles completed without undue fatigue. The pressure has lifted a lot; but who cares anyway? Up here, lying under heaven's vault listening to the choke and gurgle of the tiny stream the hullabaloo might not even exist.*

The toughest days of the trip had never caused me undue suffering until the following morning, when the inevitable psychological hangover would catch up and plunge me into misery. Despite my increased fitness this unhappy rhythm had never been dispelled, and today was no exception. Joy's firm pacing dragged me up the first of the four remaining Monar summits, Sgurr a'Chaorachain, heading straight into a gusty wind. There she left me to my own weak impetus, and returned to break camp, then make the 8-mile carry-out to the road.

Without Joy, this winter attempt would have been a folly, doomed to failure from the outset. The injury which thwarted my solo bid in 1980 was perhaps a disguised blessing and in retrospect to ever have considered going without her was naïve in the extreme. Her efforts had been unstinting, and through all the unglamorous tasks which fell to her lot she retained her enthusiasm and enjoyment of the venture. For me, each day's return was given an added thrill by her presence. There is more to living through an expedition of this duration than the animal necessities of food, warmth and a dry set of clothes every morning. But, conversely, our every parting was a little unwilling, however grand the mountains ahead, and rarely more poignant than today:

> *Thick clouds poured in from the south-west, and from Sgurr Choinnich I was struggling direct into the wind, fighting myself at the same time.*

A descent of the Allt Bealach Crudhain compelled me to a frontal attack of 700m on Lurg Mhor's north slopes. Because the peak was now thick in mist it was essential to hit the summit direct for there was a second top on the undulating ridge which could have confused the issue. On its upper section the slope moulded into a pleasant arête with a half-formed corrie on its left, but reaching the summit gave no sense of achievement, only the grave knowledge that I was a long way from home.

The ridge to Bidein a'Choire Sheasgaich was without difficulties, and by then returning to the head of Loch Monar, my route avoided its rocky north-west crest, which gives the peak a striking profile when viewed from Moruisg or Ceannaichean. The guidebooks generally advise that a traverse of Beinn Tharsuinn be taken to attain these two Munros from the north-west, but for simplicity, directness and shelter my low-level route is perhaps to be preferred, though it was by no means a smooth promenade even on a supposedly happy return and with a wind behind me:

> *A 2-mile contour, crossing innumerable streams and gullies, was needed to get to the Bealach Bhearnais and the commencement of homeward waters. My ankles were flexed to the right throughout, painfully stretching the ligaments and often turning over in the tussocks. The rain was heavy and continuous and I did it with clenched teeth, a vacant stare and a depressing vision of tomorrow's frolics on the Grey Corries. At 2.30 I reached the road but neither Joy nor the van were there.*

Oh, the woe of being soaked, dispirited and deserted; but when Joy turned up twenty minutes later she had her own tale of misfortune. On her return she found that the van's battery was flat; perhaps the lights had been left on. With the help of Gerry Howkins, who runs the private hostel at Craig, the RAC was called. They had only just succeeded in getting it started, and instead of being ready for a composed return to

Fort William, we found ourselves late, hungry, wet, very low on gas and above all disgruntled. However, Gerry came to the rescue:

'You look rough, kids,' he said. 'Come on in, I've got the water boiling for a bath.'

His huge enamel bath was filled to the brim, a pot of tea was served, and the record-player positioned outside the door to give us the magical melodies of Andean folk songs as we took our steaming dip; the third bath of the winter. Having all but crawled into the hostel, half-an-hour later we floated out, our anxieties dissolved along with the grime and sweat, and forever grateful for Gerry's kindness. We would see it through now, come what may.

Though less than two days away from the end, our routine could not be allowed to lapse. Apart from the growing pile of dirty laundry, we were as tied to the basic tasks as ever. Milk and bread were purchased at Lochcarron, and then a frantic search for the gas commenced. I wedged my foot in the door of the Dornie grocers on the stroke of its closing time at 6.30.

'Yes, we have the propane,' the lady said. Our planned cooked dinner was saved, but only just.

Then there was a string of phonecalls needed to fix my route, rendezvous points and timings; but before risking an irrevocable commitment, I wisely waited for tomorrow's weather forecast – something of a shocker, but no real surprise: 'Warm front passage... strong south-west wind, gales on coasts and hills... heavy showers...' Definitely the time for reappraisal.

A westward traverse of the Grey Corries and the Aonachs ridges, culminating in the knife edge of the Carn Mor Dearg arête, is the finest walker's route by which to approach Ben Nevis. Starting from Luibeilt bothy at the eastern end, 9,000ft of ascent are required to reach the Ben, an arduous day in itself, and in winter a serious expedition, Aonach Beag in particular having a notorious reputation. Thoroughly comparable to the Mamores Ridge in quality, it possesses the extra stature of leading to Britain's highest summit as well as its greatest precipice, and gives a crescendo of height and scenic magnificence; indeed, the grandest possible conclusion to the winter Munros.

However, in light of the forecast this plan posed twin problems – the difficulty, even the impossibility, of walking straight into the gale, and the necessity of a bivouac somewhere around the Aonachs. My route had first to make a 10-mile crossing of Sgurr Eilde Mor and Binnein

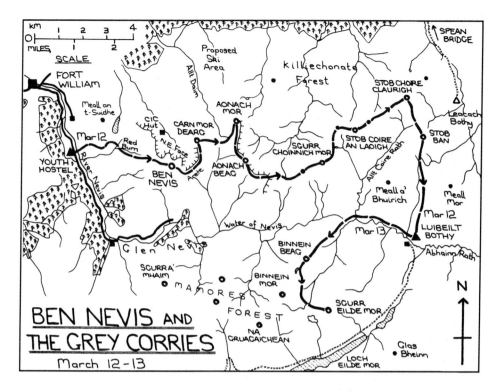

BEN NEVIS AND THE GREY CORRIES

March 12-13

Beag even to reach the Luibeilt steading, which is the last available accommodation before the Ben itself. Yet in order to finish by mid-morning on the thirteenth it was essential to press on from here to within four hours' striking distance of the end.

The implications were clear enough to me: a heavy sack with overnight gear... fighting the wind to exhaustion... soaked by the rain... a blizzard on the high tops... and *then* an open bivouac at 700 or 800m. Not a chance. Fame is one thing, but martyrdom is quite another story! Yet turning the picture round, a different tale emerged: go west–east starting with the Ben... hardest section first... blown along the Grey Corries... no bivouac pack... meet Joy for a warm dry night at Luibeilt and finish at a canter onto Sgurr Eilde Mor.

The rationale was, however, lost on our publicity organisers, Thomson and Bonnist, and the change of mind was met with dismay and acrimony:

'You'll lose all the impact.'

'No one's ever heard of Sgurr Eilde Mor.'

'The press were all planning to climb the Ben, even the TV men... we can't change now...'

But they failed to budge me, and were left in the panic of rearrangement while we drove on to our last overnight park in Glen Nevis, my goodwill soured by their seeming lack of consideration of the trials we were going through to finish on time, whatever the route taken. My obstinacy also stemmed from growing disillusionment over the supposed purpose of the publicity – to raise money for Intermediate Technology. Yet for all this puppet show, a paltry £2,000 had so far been received. Was it really worth the fuss?

But the very obscurity of the chosen finishing peak possessed its own appeal, and was perhaps more fitting to the experience of the past three months. The popular image still exists that there are no worthy mountains in Scotland besides Ben Nevis, the Cairngorms and the peaks of Glencoe. My express intent this winter had been to explore the wealth of fine Munros outside these glamour spots; and equally to see the most barren and bleakest places, to absorb their strange beauty and cope with their loneliness. So Sgurr Eilde Mor would do very nicely to symbolise this spirit, and perhaps might help to break the myth. But its summit crown was still ten Munros away, and the last week had taught me the one good lesson that nothing can ever be taken for granted.

At 6.45 I set off into a gloomy dawn which morbidly foretold the day to come. Alan Thomson joined me but soon turned back; this was not the light for his photographs and I was hardly inclined to stop for them anyway. Through the winter Alan and I had built a productive working relationship and, more importantly, a happy companionship in our days on the hills. It was a pity that the conflicting demands of publicity and good mountaineering sense should have slightly tarnished the fruition of our efforts. Alan Hinkes came up to help me find the summit, but thereon it was back to my own company.

The 'pony track' to the top of Ben Nevis is the biggest and the most popular ascent in the Highlands, but is probably unrivalled in its tedium, and in winter there is a vicious sting to its tail whenever the mists are down. The benign security of the broad zig-zags is abruptly relinquished as they disappear under the snowfields. One suddenly remembers the two who died in January's avalanche on these simple slopes, and then debouching onto the summit plateau the jagged indents of the north-east face shave perilously close to the line of travel. In this morning's thick cloud and light snowfall the last half mile was a tense affair even though Alan and I between us had climbed all the gullies and faces we sought to avoid.

It seems uncanny that climbers emerging from grade V verticalities can then fail to find the tourist descent. Over-prudence is the usual error; steering too wide a course away from the northern cliffs, and in so doing wandering into the chasms on the western flanks where Five Finger and Surgeon's Gullies are the usual snares. However, the tenuous navigation needed to get off the top in a white-out adds to the challenge and rewards of climbing on the north face.

Whatever the Aberdonians claim for their beloved Cairngorms, it is the Ben which gives the most reliable winter climbing conditions by virtue of its extra height, scale and humidity, especially for the majority to whom 'good' conditions mean solid, well plated ice rather than the snowed-up rock to which the devotees of Lochnagar are so partial. Even during this snowless winter the great Point Five and Zero Gullies had developed magnificent ribbons of ice, and doubtless had been especially crowded by climbers, due to the bareness of the adjoining faces and the poor fare in Glencoe.

The summit shelter was encrusted by rime ice, maybe not in the proportions of the 7-foot daggers that were once noted sticking out of the observatory anemometer in the last century, but wintry none the less. Careful bearings were now required, for the descent of the south-east ridge onto the Carn Mor Dearg arête is the most treacherous on the mountain. On the left the slope assumes a gradually steepening convexity, which can entice the unwary to a premature plunge over the Coire Leis headwall.

The arête was free of ice, but covered with loose snow. Its graceful sweep was missed, likewise the close-up study of Nevis's great buttresses which are revealed as the corrie head is turned. Today the edge was merely an extended trial of care and patience, thankfully quitted for the easier ground of Carn Mor Dearg's eastern spur, which gives the link to the two Aonachs:

> I sheltered by the ruined wall on the col and ate a cheese sandwich. So far, so good; conditions had been colder and less windy than expected. An ice-blue window appeared in the cloud, raising hopes to an unwarranted pitch...

This was the first and last sight of the sky. The following climb took me back in the clouds and onto the belly-shaped top of Aonach Mor. Its rough pile of granite stones now guards a heath of lonely desolation, but ten years hence perhaps it will be thrice the size and mobbed by swarms of roving walkers who have dismounted from the proposed gondola lifts to trek into the imagined 'wilderness', much in the mode of a second Cairn Gorm. The 'honeypot' style of development is seen by many as the saviour of the remaining remote tracts; but the sacrifice of Aonach Mor and its hinterland is a heavy price to pay.

As I crept about the bald head of Aonach Beag checking for the highest point, a gusting wind and penetrating sleet commenced. Quickly my spectacles were fogged over and blurred, and so my gropings became tense and unsure. A tiny cairn is rumoured to exist on the top, and many minutes were spent teetering close to the cornice dollops on the eastern edge to prove that it was either a myth or else in hibernation. The extremes of lunacy which the aspirant Munroist will endure! But my own affliction was soon to be cured; just six to go.

Finding the continuing ridge to the Grey Corries brought greater problems:

> The eastern face was one long débâcle without any clear offshoot to tempt me. I spent half an hour wandering back and forth along the edge, losing confidence and getting cold. On realising that my indecision could be a symptom of mild exposure, I plumped for a steep snow wall close to the compass line, and a further 50m of awkward scrambling led onto easier ground and a ridge of sorts. Shivering noticeably now I stopped immediately to put on all spare clothes and ate the rest of my food. It was 2.30, and there were 6 miles still to go above the 850m level. Time was short; I had to push on, but would I warm up again?

Fortunes rose as soon as the characteristic quartzite screes of the Grey Corries were underfoot. With an increased pace on the easy ridge over Sgurr Choinnich Mor the warmth flooded back, and though battered this way and that by a furious wind, the doubt of finishing evaporated. Occasionally the rain would cease and the gale tore the clouds apart giving wild views of the twisting ridge ahead.

> I was on Stob Choire Claurigh just before 5pm, which gave two hours till darkness. Only the detached subsidiary of Stob Ban remained, a 130m scarp of shattered scree. I crawled up, buckled against the wind and now tiring rapidly, but in quite triumphant mood. It had been a tough battle but at last I knew I could complete the Munros.

The rain became more persistent on the boggy descent to Luibeilt, and darkness came early. At 7pm I opened the bothy door. Joy was slightly concerned, for my arrival was an hour overdue, and this was not a good night for an enforced bivouac. My dripping clothes joined her own on the wires above the fire. There were two others at the bothy very much keeping to their own company, so we were unable to vent our many thoughts. Once warmed and fed we ensconced ourselves in a quiet night of contemplation while the storm rattled on outside.

Inevitably there was excited anticipation, especially for Joy:

> *In a few hours a hot bath and a change of clothes were in prospect – a chance to be a little more feminine. But also I felt sad that this strange existence was to be broken. Would we simply drop into a mental vacuum after striving for so long? The idea of returning to the city left me feeling empty and depressed. Far from having missed our former existence, the cosy convenience of suburban life has lost all appeal, and until we have settled ourselves permanently in the Highlands I won't rest happy.*

And likewise myself. No exploit in the mountains ever seems to leave the heart at rest, and the Munros were no exception. The direction, style and location may alter, but a love of wild places and the search for their challenge seems only to be increased by hard experience. Devotion or addiction, call it what you will.

Above all, the winter mountains had given a lasting happiness, 83 days that will never be erased from the memory. True, we had remarkable luck in selecting the least windy and snowy season for over a decade, which had helped me to finish a week within the schedule. Compared to the expected 42 days with gales on the summits, my records totalled only 26, whilst precipitation was on average three-quarters of its normal level*. So we had far more than our ration of sunshine and frost. But the great tempests also possess their own awesome appeal, and epics like today's on the Grey Corries will perhaps be the most cherished of all. Indeed, the relative absence of snow and storm was one of my slight disappointments of this 1985 winter.

Doing the Munros in a single winter had been a self-motivated adventure, but how would the achievement stand, stripped of the public glory and assessed on its true merits? The thought was of special concern as we approached the end. Certainly a new record had been created for the fastest completion of the peaks, though the tactics and season were not comparable to anything that had gone before. But its only wider significance, and the real measure of its impact, is whether

---

*See Appendix IV for detailed weather statistics.

it motivates others to new challenges, just as Hamish's walk had inspired my own idea.

A continuous journey without motor assistance in the ninety days was far beyond my own capability or conception, but by allowing a full four months from 1 December to 31 March a non-stop winter walk is feasible. And eventually somebody with supreme fortitude, skill and a slice of luck, may overcome the hazards and do this within the calendar season. Then, looking to the summer, the time is overdue for a fell-running attempt*. The remarkable feats achieved in the Lake District, Pennines and increasingly in Scotland have shown that there are several men of the necessary calibre – seventy-five days, or even less? And nor should Corbett's 221 peaks above 2,500ft be ignored, for here is an odyssey which would take one from the Border hills to the Outer Isles**. An overdose of 'Munrosis' can blinker the sights to the vast variety and extent of Scotland's lower hills.

But, apart from these extreme endeavours, I hope that as great a stimulus may be provided to those with modest ambitions, or who enjoy the hills in a relaxed fashion, and especially those who presently confine their visits to the lighter seasons of the year. Winter demands a greater respect, prudence and preparedness, but please go and seek, for the pleasures should not be denied and the mountains are still so empty.

At 6am we struggled into damp clothes and stumbled out into a cooler, fresher morning – the usual gruelling ritual of warming up and setting a pace. The hills were lightly dusted with overnight snow, and the dew rose up the grasses to freeze at the touch of the north-west breeze. The thought that I might have bivouacked on Aonach Beag produced a shudder. Both it and Ben Nevis were still clamped under the cloud.

Up on Binnein Beag a feral cat loped across the screes not 50m above us, a lucky sighting which enlivened the toilsome slog from the Glen Nevis watershed. For some reason we were dragging our feet. As the

---

* Since 1995 there have been several continuous journeys by top-class fell-runners, the fastest round completed entirely on foot taking just 67 days (see Appendix V for full details).

** As this was written, twenty-five-year-old Craig Caldwell was three-quarters of the way through a prolonged attempt to combine all the Munros and Corbetts in a single journey – an effort plagued by the wettest summer since 1897 (see Appendix V for details).

morning haze dissolved, the string of streams and lochans over to the east sparkled into our sight. The air was crystal clear, and pausing on the top we filled our lungs with glad and generous draughts.

Twisting around the shoulder of Binnein Mor by the stalking track and onto the ridge of Sgurr Eilde Mor already we could spot a few figures moving about on its summit, so our finish was not to go unseen. Just 200m to go up the screes and snowbanks above the ice-choked lochan; it was a pity to have to stop...

POSTSCRIPT

The cruel fact of life that success counts for all was amply proven on our completion. During the next nine months our appeal total for Intermediate Technology multiplied to £20,000, and through articles, lectures and broadcasts the charity was given a wealth of additional promotion. So the stress and pressure of the publicity (which had some-times taxed us more than the Munros themselves!) was worthwhile, even though the amount is a drop in an ocean of need.

APPENDIX I

GLOSSARY

Heights and Distances

The alternating use of the metric and imperial scales in the book deserves an apology and a brief explanation. All long distances are given in miles to provide a consistent measure in line with traditional convention. However, metrication has been attempted in the case of heights. Whilst Munros are defined by their height in feet, the Ordnance Survey maps are now fully metric in scale, contour intervals and all heights. The dilemma was insoluble, and a compromise has been struck by quoting all height intervals on the ground and summit altitudes in metres, but quoting daily total ascents in both numbers of metres and feet. The outrageous suggestion (no doubt made with 'tongue in cheek') has been heard from some quarters that with metrication Munros are outdated and should be replaced by a list of 'Metros' (peaks over either 900 or 1,000 metres in altitudes). Given the current boom in the Munros cult, there is scant chance that this idea will ever gain acceptance.

Winter Climbing Grades

Graded climbs on *snow and ice* in Scotland are now grouped into eight classes:

   I   Uncomplicated average-angled snow climbs having no pitches normally. May however have cornice difficulties or dangerous runouts.

  II   Gullies which contain either individual or minor pitches or high-angled snow with difficult cornice exits. The easier buttresses (ie, Moderate in Summer) under winter conditions.

 III   Gullies which contain ice in quantity. There will normally be at least one substantial pitch and possibly several lesser ones. Sustained buttress climbs (ie Difficult in Summer) but only technical in short sections.

 IV   Steeper than grade III and of higher technical difficulty. Vertical sections may be expected on ice climbs, and buttresses will require a good repertoire of techniques.

  V   Difficult, sustained and serious climbs. If on ice, long sustained ice pitches are to be expected; buttress routes will require a degree of rock-climbing ability and the use of axe hooking and torquing techniques.

VI, VII and VIII The hardest ice and buttress climbs.

For pure *rock* climbing the traditional British gradings are used where required in the text. These are: Easy, Moderate, Difficult, Very Difficult, Severe, Very Severe, Hard Very Severe, Extremely Severe.

Gaelic Glossary

The reader is referred to the excellent 'Gaelic Guide' in the 1990 edition of *Munro's Tables* (Scottish Mountaineering Club) for an introduction to Gaelic grammar, a list of commonly used names, a phonetic key, and the complete translation and pronunciation of all the Munros' names. Rather than inadequately trying to replicate the scholarship of this Guide, only the most common names for topographical features which recur in the text are listed below, as an immediate aid to the geographical understanding of the mountains, and it is hoped the enjoyment of the book.

abhainn	stream	*glas, ghlas*	grey, greenish-grey, green
allt	stream, burn		
aonach	mountain ridge, hill, moor	*gorm*	blue, (of grass) green
		lairig	pass
ban	white, light-coloured	*liath*	grey, bluish grey
beag	small	*lochan*	small lake, tarn
bealach	pass	*mam*	large rounded hill
beinn,		*maol*	bald, bare
bheinn bein	hill, mountain	*meadhoin,*	
bidean,		*mheadhoin*	middle
bidein	peak, summit	*meall*	rounded hill
binnein	pointed peak	*monadh*	moor, range; hill, mountain
buidhe	yellow		
caorann,		*mor,*	
chaorainn	rowan tree	*mhor (more)*	big
carn, cairn	heap of stones, cairn-shaped hill	*mullach*	summit, top
		odhar,	
clach	stone	*odhair*	fawnish brown
coille	wood	*riabhach*	brindled, greyish
coire, choire	corrie, glaciated valley (literally a cauldron, kettle)	*ruadh*	red, red-brown
		sail	rounded hill
		sgur(r),	
creag	rock, crag	*sgor(r)*	rocky hill or peak
cruach	stack-shaped hill	*spidean*	peak, summit
dearg	red	*sron*	jutting ridge
dubh	black	*stac, stuc*	steep conical hill
eas	waterfall	*stob*	pointed hill
fionn	white, pale coloured	*tarsuinn*	transverse, (a) cross
gabhar,		*toll*	hole, hollow
ghabhar	goat	*tom*	small rounded hill
garbh	rough	*uamh*	cave
geal	white	*uisge*	water

NB See Bibliography for suggested further reading and the address of Intermediate Technology

ROUTE STATISTICS

An estimated total of 1,028 map miles of walking and 125,580m (412,000ft) of ascent was required to complete the Munros, an average of 12.4 miles and 1,515m (4,965ft) for each of the 83 days, or 13.9 miles and 1,700m (5,570ft) for the 74 active days, excluding those spent in rest or stormbound. This tallied very closely to my planning estimates. The analysis of daily mileages and ascents shows how varied the itineraries were in their length and duration:

Miles per day	Days	Ascent per day (x 1,000ft)	Days
Rest Days	9	Rest Days	9
5–10	20	Less than 3	7
10–15	23	3–4	1 1
15–20	17	4–5	15
20–25	12	5–6	7
Over 25	2	6–7	17
		7–8	9
		8–9	4
		9–10	2
		Over 10	2

The daily scores of Munros were likewise widely scattered:

Munros per day	Days	Munros per day	Days
0	10	5	12
1	10	6	5
2	14	7	2
3	12	8	3
4	12	9	3

Joy's final total of Munros on the trip was 120.

The response to the 67 brochures left on the tops was expectedly patchy. Only 21 were returned as requested, and the discovery of a further 2 was proven by way of an irate letter sent to one of the magazines. Of the remainder, it may be assumed that many disintegrated during their weeks of burial in the summit cairns, or else the handwritten request for their return washed off. Happily, 11 of those returned were accompanied by a donation, giving a welcome total of £100 towards our appeal for IT. The longest known survivor was that left on Carn Dearg in Ben Alder Forest, deposited on 12 January and extracted by Tim Young of Cumbria on 29 March.

EQUIPMENT, DIET AND HEALTH

Note: Readers should be aware that many of the makes and models of equipment described in this section are no longer in manufacture.

Equipment and Clothing

The motto for the success of the Munros venture was to travel light and fast. Yet this ethic had to be harnessed to the equal necessity of being fully clothed and equipped to survive the worst imaginable weather. The compromise between these conflicting objectives lay in 'quality'. By selecting lightweight items of high performance and durability to cover the essential needs, quantity and bulk could be minimised.

Travelling alone for much of the time necessitated an attitude of total self-reliance. In the event of a mishap, no rescue or assistance could be anticipated, and indeed would not have been wished for except in the direst hour of need, so each day's rucksac contained the following items which were considered essential to *prevent* as well as *endure* an unplanned bivouac.

Ice axe (curved pick) and crampons (front-pointed) These items were *never* left behind (though the sharing arrangement on the Cuillin was a regrettable miscalculation, see Ch 14). With the confidence of experience, I knew I could tackle steep ground of up to grade III with just these two items in event of a route-finding disaster. The axe is quite sufficient to fashion an emergency snowhole. Spare crampon strap, rivets and adjusters were also carried.
Headtorch Including spare battery and bulbs.
Bivouac sac Full-length nylon/goretex with zipped hood, weighing little over ¹/₂kg.
First-aid kit Including sufficient bandaging, tape and gauze to cope with a major trauma; painkillers (DF 118).
Food The day's lunch (see Diet) plus a couple of spare energy food bars; usually a total of 1,800 calories.
Map and compass A plastic wallet gave excellent protection against rapid disintegration in wind or rain; if possessed, a spare map was carried (see Ch 12).
Snow goggles Only taken on the skiing days when snow glare was dangerously strong, or when blizzards were likely.
Rucksac Berghaus Redpoint 'Red Wall' – lightweight, with padded-foam back for seat insulation on a bivouac or bothy stay. Nylon bivouac extension above the knees also available.

Spare mittens, wool balaclava, long johns and thin sweater (see Personal Clothing) .

Several people expressed surprise that Joy and I did not carry two-way radios to maintain contact and co-ordination. My personal view is that such paraphernalia are an unwanted encumbrance, detracting from the freedom and simplicity of mountaineering. They might have caused more confusion than clarification, especially in times of self doubt when I could easily have been tempted by Joy's voice to abandon a day. In any event, radios would have added little to the 'telepathic' understanding which linked us almost faultlessly throughout the expedition.

With a genuine pang of guilt I must admit that the porterage of the extra equipment for overnight stays at bothies was not usually my concern! However, suffice to say that the usual requisites of sleeping bag, gaz stove, pan, spare socks and vest, candle, firelighter, matches and utensils were carried. 'Epigas' screw-in gas canisters gave long-lasting fuel supply at a sustained pressure; but it is wise to check that cartridge and burner are compatible and the seal valves are working before embarking into the wilderness with them, given our experience in Ben Alder Forest (Ch 5). On the occasions when I did carry a full overnight pack (eg, Knoydart, Cairngorms, Glen Tilt) the total burden was never greater than 12kg.

Personal Clothing

This was of course my most important insurance against the elements, and, having found a combination that served me well, my dress was rarely varied. However the kit as listed below, whilst fine for the continuously moving hillwalker, might be found insufficient for the roped ice climber who spends so much of his day waiting and shivering on belay stances.

Boots Medium weight, half-stiffened leather boots were worn throughout – mainly Scarpa Trionic SL, but occasionally Scarpa Manta, the latter proving lighter and more comfortable. The boots coped with all terrain from frontpointing on steep snow, to rock scrambling, and jogging on tracks and roads. They did not wear appreciably on the soles (but this is to have been expected when so much of the walking was on frozen ground and snow).

Gaiters Berghaus Yeti Gaiters (with rubber rand on the welt) ensured warm dry feet on nearly every day. However, the rubbers wore out with distressing rapidity, and had to be re-randed several times. By using strong adhesive (eg, 'Superglue') to stick down the toes, the durability was improved to around 3 weeks. It must be remembered, however, that they were being given the roughest possible treatment, often on loose rocky ground. For pure snow and ice climbing, or boggy walking, the Yetis are ideal (if expensive) and they also of course protect the boot uppers from wear.

Jacket A lined goretex anorak (with hood) seems the perfect outer garment for fast travel in the Scottish winter. Down-filled jackets are too warm for all but the most severe conditions, and therefore prone to cause excess sweating (with subsequent chilling and energy loss). They are also rendered ineffective when wetted, as so often happens on the winter mountains. Our own Thinsulate-filled jackets only became essential on the days on the Feshie hills during the −30°C windstorm. Otherwise, my Stormbelt Jacket (goretex with a towelling lining) proved warm, windproof and watertight in all conditions. The 'breathability' of the outer material, and the absorption quality of the towelling kept my inner garments fairly dry even when working hard.

Salopettes Stretch-cotton salopettes (French make) were warm, comfortable and very quick drying. By contrast, the Rohan 'SuperSalopettes' (in thicker stretch Helenca) which were occasionally worn, usually proved too hot and heavy for quick travel and are better for serious climbing. With the potential addition of long johns and overtrousers, a light salopette is far more adaptable to the wide range of conditions. However, salopettes have been very slow to gain favour in Britain especially among hillwalkers who seem loathe to discard traditional breeches. In my view these give the problems of heat loss and discomfort at the midriff, together with exposed kneecaps if they are cut too short. However, ladies may have their own reason to disagree with this recommendation!

Overtrousers Goretex, with waist drawcord to prevent excessive sagging, and full-length side zips enabling them to be donned or removed when wearing crampons.

Gloves/mittens and wool balaclava Keeping the extremities warm was of the greatest concern – frozen hands are unable to cope with the simplest tasks, whilst the heat-loss through an exposed cranium is enormous. Spares were always carried. Fur-lined goretex covered mitts were very warm though by no means waterproof; wool Dachstein mitts proved equally warm and retained their insulation better when wet. Sewn wrist-loops guarded against loss when temporarily removed. Thin inner gloves were also carried but rarely worn, mitts providing a better core of heat and keeping the fingers together.

Long johns (Helly Hansen) Only worn on the very coldest days but usually carried.

Fibrepile jacket Remarkably this was often not needed, so efficient was the outer Stormbelt jacket.

Other items Thin spare sweater, wool shirt, long-sleeved vest, ski hat.

Nordic Ski Equipment

This was only used for six days on the expedition, whereas at least a fortnight had been hoped and expected. Our chosen combination of kit, whilst not thoroughly tested, proved light, efficient and ideally suited to the Scottish hill terrain:

Skis Kneissel White Star, 210cm, metal edged, waxable (Martin); Trak Telemark 205cm, metal edged, fishscale bottomed (Joy). The fishscale tread

proved ineffective on slopes in excess of 15°, especially on hard or icy snow.
Bindings 3-pin Rottefeller.
Boots Asolo (Snowfield); very warm, vibram soled, and could be fitted to
crampons and Yeti gaiters; adaptable to mixed climbing and skiing terrain.
Skins Brushed nylon; excellent for long or steep climbs.
Other items Poles, waxing kit (though not used on the hill owing to lack of
time and expertise), spare-pole basket, screwdriver and repair kit, spare skin.

Camera

Finally, my camera cannot be passed without mention. It was an ever-present
companion demanding frequent stops and continual exposure no matter how
severe the weather or short the daylight; in use the bane of my life, but with
retrospect, and a collection of some 750 slides to illustrate our memory of the
trip, an indispensable accoutrement. A Minolta X300 (35mm SLR) was
purchased for the trip, with a choice between a standard 50mm lens and a
28mm wideangle, with which a simple UV filter was used continuously. Apart
from the malfunction mentioned in Ch 2 which was due entirely to my own
ineptitude, and an occasional falter in the batteries at −15°C and below, the
camera operated excellently all winter. With a padded pouch and shoulder
sling it was well protected and easily portable. Kodachrome 64 and Fuji 100
films were used alternately, the former giving admirable reproduction of pure
snowscapes, whilst the Fuji better captured the complete colour contrast from
the greens and browns of the glens to the snowy summits.

Diet

The abnormal duration of the expedition coupled with the continual exposure
to the cold made our diet of the prime concern. A high daily calorific intake
was an obvious prerequisite but a properly balanced intake of all vitamins and
minerals is equally essential to sustain an effort through 90 days. Neither a
short-term depletion of immediate energy, nor a long-term physical run-down
due to a lack of nutrients could be entertained. One dose of exhaustion in
severe conditions might have spelt the end of the venture, to say nothing of
me, especially given the tenuous thread of our lightweight strategy.

The long-term problem seems to have affected several previous Scottish
marathons. In 1967 the Ripley brothers abandoned the first attempt on the
continuous Munros round just 50 peaks from the end, reportedly in an
advanced state of bodily exhaustion and malnutrition; whilst in 1984 Rick
Ansell was so plagued by hunger on his nonstop walk of the mainland Munros
that he was driven to searching for discarded 'half-eaten butties' around the
summit cairns. Coming off Beinn Sgulaird, Rick was convinced of suffering
hallucinations from hunger when an apple, a cake and three Opal Fruits
appeared on the side of the track with the sign 'Please Eat' attached, but amaz-

ingly this wayside offering proved genuine and was promptly devoured.

On a non-stop walk it is naturally difficult to ensure a continuous supply of wholesome groceries, especially when they have to be carried on the back, but it is my strong suspicion that far too many walkers rely on dried, processed and prepackaged food to the exclusion of all else, and hence accelerate their dietary downfall. Dried food especially is squeezed and drained of its goodness, and has the reputation of exercising little else apart from the bowels, which in itself depletes the body's reserves.

With the use of transport there was certainly no excuse for our failing to visit the Highland village stores regularly, and Joy made the most strenuous efforts to procure fresh food stocks at every stage of our journey. Fresh fruit, milk and vegetables even featured on the bothy menu on occasions, and never once was a packet of dried stew or curry opened for our main meal, for which I give thanks, as eating surely is an enjoyment as well as a necessity.

Neither of us eat meat, and so we relied on fish, nuts and pulses (especially lentils) for our protein supply. The content of the diet was deliberately biased away from glucose. On a prolonged test of endurance one requires a 'slow, steady and sustained' stream of energy rather than the short-lived boosts provided by pure sweets and sugar, which can leave the body feeling even more depleted in their aftermath. Basic fats and carbohydrates are far more appropriate sources of calories.

A typical menu for one of the tougher days of the trip (ie, greater than 15 miles, 6,000ft) is given below, with calories per meal, as the best means of summarising our diet. On easier days the calorie intake might drop to 3,250 as a minimum. With no oven and only two gas rings and a grill at our disposal Joy found a pressure cooker indispensable to maintain invention and variety.

Breakfast (700 calories)
Stewed prunes
Muesli, banana, milk
Toast, margarine and honey (2 rounds)
Tea

Lunch/Hill Food (1,500 calories)
Cheese and wholemeal bread sandwich
Flask of hot soup or drinking chocolate
Slice of fruit cake, fresh apple
2 'Crunchy' Bars (oats/almonds/honey)
Bar of fudge and/or chocolate

Dinner (1,650 calories)
Grilled grapefruit
Lentil and nut cakes
Cheese and garlic potatoes
Fried cabbage
Steamed apple sponge, cream or yogurt

Bedtime (150 calories)
Cup of drinking chocolate
Piece of fresh fruit

TOTAL FOR DAY: 4,000 calories

On the bothy trips the usual menu comprised:

Breakfast (500 calories)
Muesli, hot milk, dried fruit, sugar
Wholemeal biscuits, margarine and honey
Tea

Lunch (1,700 calories)
As normal but with extra energy bars

Dinner (1,400 calories)
Soup and oatcakes
125gm spaghetti, margarine, tinned tuna, cheese, fresh fried onion and garlic
Custard and dried apples or apricots
Tea and powdered orange drink

TOTAL FOR DAY: 3,600 calories

Health

The success of this diet was clearly manifested in our maintaining a clean bill of health, except for Joy's head cold, throughout the trip. Happily not a single aspirin, sleeping tablet, vitamin pill, iron booster or any other supplement passed our lips during the 83 days. The outdoor existence certainly proved to be a healthy way, but perhaps the fact of our living in a glorified refrigerator and quite apart from the rest of humanity also explains this apparent immunity to infection.

Remarkably, I finished the Munros at exactly the same weight with which the journey was commenced, just under $10^1/_2$ stone. This is perhaps the best testimony to the accuracy of Joy's provisioning. A rapid weight loss was something to be feared, for though invigorating in the short-term it would have left me with precious little fat or muscle reserves for an emergency. Therefore I was deliberately indulgent in my eating, even on the very rare occasions when an appetite was lacking. However, within my constant total weight something like a stone must have been transferred from my top half down to the legs, as was evident when I found myself hanging by the arms trying to rock climb again in the spring!

The serious doubts over the fortitude of my much abused knees and ankles on commencing the trip proved needless. By taking due care to avoid excessive jarring on the joints especially early in the day when not warmed up, and on the long steep descents, no problems were encountered, and a build-up of muscles in the appropriate places compensated for my torn and strained ligaments. In fact the continuous activity seemed to do these ailments a power of good. Stiffness and fluid accumulation, usually so noticeable when at my sedentary accountancy job, magically disappeared.

A careful routine prevented other potentially disabling maladies. Nightly washing, a coat of talcum powder and clean socks kept the feet warm, healthy and blister-free. The only recurrently painful nuisance was the finger chilblains which seem to germinate excellently in the alternating hot and cold environments.

A good level of general fitness was attained after the expected struggles of the first ten days, and well sustained thereafter. However, the occasional rest days gave a tremendous boost to my energies, especially when I was flagging after a string of hard outings. The varying of daily mileage and ascent was found to be not only a wise concession to the fluxes of weather, but also an ideal regime for maintaining physical freshness, an adaptability between speed and endurance, and most vitally a keen mental interest throughout the expedition.

WINTER MOUNTAIN WEATHER AND SNOW CONDITIONS

Not surprisingly, we maintained a vested interest in the weather throughout the winter, for the final fate of the Munros' attempt lay firmly in the lap of the Gods, however great my endeavour or skilled our tactics. This element of chance was indeed one of the most appealing aspects of the expedition. We set off without an inkling of what was coming. Three months of snow and frost, or rain and gale – either possibility had to be faced with equanimity, for unpredictability and turbulence make Highland winter weather an impossible beast to tame.

Each day's forecast was therefore awaited with bated breath, and like a pair of hawks we scanned the skies for the slightest portent of a change in conditions. As part of this interest I kept regular daily records of the mountain weather features, mainly based on visual observations, for here was a unique chance to obtain a complete picture of a winter on the hills, there being few climbers who are out on the tops on *every* day of the season.

By publishing my observations, together with supplementary data from the Meteorological Office stations, and the Cairn Gorm summit Automatic Weather Station (AWS) both from 1984/85, and for previous years, it is hoped to contribute to three important aims.

(i) The accumulation of a *pool of weather data* for the mountain summits in winter as a source of information to all hillgoers.
(ii) To assist the understanding of *synoptic weather maps* and forecasts, and especially their interpretation into the likely conditions that will be encountered on the mountains given the prevailing pattern of pressure, and airmass movements.
(iii) To show the link between the patterns of weather and the changes in snow type, depth and quality on the hills, especially in the prediction of good climbing conditions and of *avalanche risk*.

Undoubtedly there is a paramount need for an increased knowledge among climbers of all three aspects, particularly in winter and especially for the leaders of young or inexperienced parties.

The intending hillgoer is currently supplied with a plethora of weather information, much of which is irrelevant, or else requires a certain technical knowledge to interpret correctly. General weather forecasts are especially dangerous if digested without modification, for they try to reproduce the likely conditions at low-level altitudes and give little indication of the greater severity of climate higher up. Also they tend to be definitive, giving little idea of the possible *range* of conditions that could be faced, and this is where the weather chart offers a much broader picture, *if* it can be understood.

So the climber has to make a rather tricky translation of all this data to predict the happenings in the high corries or on the Munro summits. In summer if his prejudgement is widely amiss, a minor epic, a retreat or an unwanted wetting may ensue, the sort of experience that is part of the fun of the sport! In winter, when conditions can quickly pass beyond the threshold of physical tolerance, the same error may result in a battle for survival. And also in winter the 'translation' problem is more complex, for it must take account of freezing levels, and the type of snow that might fall, or has fallen – witness our own failure to anticipate the white blanket on the Cuillin Ridge.

Awareness of these imperatives has increased in recent years, though it required several tragedies to arouse a proper concern. Since the closure of the Ben Nevis summit Observatory in 1904, mountain weather recording was highly fragmentary until in 1977 the Cairn Gorm AWS commenced operation. With the help of the data from Cairn Gorm and with the operation of Scottish Avalanche Information Service to give daily snow reports from Glencoe, Lochaber, Creag Meagaidh, Northern Cairngorms and Lochnagar, there are now several forecasts available specifically for mountaineers. Avalanche reports for the five areas are currently available on freephone/fax 0800 987988 and the Climbline weather forecasts can be obtained on 0891 654669 (West Highlands) and 0891 654668 (East Highlands). However, we still found the specialist forecasts to be widely awry on several occasions, most notably during the February windstorm on Cairn Gorm.

At the outset it must be stressed that apart from temperature readings, my own observations were wholly subjective, and were also of course highly 'mobile' – my experience on Ben Hope would hardly provide an accurate indicator of events on Ben Lomond 200 miles to the south; but wherever possible other data has been used to consolidate an average picture across the country, and better a rough sketch than none at all!

The climate of the 1984/1985 winter confounded my gloomiest anticipations. Stable continental and polar airmasses were predominant, and denied the westerly airstream its usual influence. This makes the supplement of average comparatives for previous periods especially vital. Never should our lucky experience be taken as a model for future years!

Temperature

The prevalence of Arctic and land-cooled continental airstreams produced a colder than average winter in 1984/85. There is still the misconception among many that the colder the weather the more severe and dangerous it is, but in fact the opposite holds more truth. Especially given the excellent insulation of modern boots and clothing, pure cold is not to be feared to the same degree as the wind, and especially a gale combined with a wet snowfall and a temperature hovering on zero, which produces a more immediate wetting, loss of insulation and consequent chilling of the body.

Table 1 shows that the depression of temperature was experienced on both the east and west sides of the country, especially in January when we recorded 21 successive nights with frost from 1st to 21st, and a winter minimum of −16°C at Newtonmore on the 24th–25th. Braemar's winter minimum of −22.7° came two nights later (when we were in the warmer west at Glencoe). The anticyclonic persistence throughout this period was highly unusual, for a stormy (and therefore warmer) early January is one of the major singularities of the seasonal weather cycles in the Highlands.

By comparison, our highest overnight minimum was +10°C at Inchnadamph on 22–23 February, when the great rainstorm commenced. Indeed, average temperature figures hide the marked variation between periods of westerly and easterly airstream dominance. Roughly ordering the daily situations between the two categories, 40 days of Atlantic low-pressure airflow were discerned with a mean minimum of +2.6°, and 43 days of Polar/continental high-pressure dominance with a mean of −3.6°.

The mountaineer must be especially vigilant for the rapid fluxes of temperature which accompany a switch in airstream and which can create great instability in the snow cover. A blizzard which begins cold and ends warm can lay down an undercoat of loose powder pellets beneath a topping of heavy wet flakes producing a snow profile in imminent danger of collapse. Conversely, a rapid thaw can cause an immediate risk of wet snowslide and cornice collapse. For instance, during 27 and 28 January, Braemar's temperature rocketed from −17.9° to +5.7°.

Table 1 Minimum Daily Air Temperature (°C), Monthly Means

	Braemer (339 metres)	Onich (15 metres) (nr Ballachulish)	Own Readings (170 metres average)
Dec 1984	−0.1	2.6	2.1 (21st–31st)
1951–80 average	−0.9	−1.9	−
Difference from average	+0.8	+0.7	−
Jan 1985	−4.8	−1.7	−2.8
1951–80 average	−2.5	0.9	−
Difference from average	−2.3	−2.6	−

Feb	1985	−3.7	−0.1	−1.6
	1951–80 average	−3.1	0.5	−
	Difference from average−0.6		−0.6	−
Mar	1985	−1.7	1.2	3.9
				(1st–13th)
	1951–80 average	−0.9	2.0	−
	Difference from average−0.8		−0.8	−
4 month Means	1984/85	−2.6	0.5	−0.7
	1951–80 average	−1.9	1.3	−
	Difference from average−0.7		−0.8	−

(*Source:* Meteorological Office, Edinburgh)

Conversion of valley temperatures to summit altitudes using the simple lapse rate of 0.64°C per 100 metres is inapplicable owing to the prevalence of night-time inversions during anticyclones.

Table 2 Cairn Gorm Summit Temperatures (°C)

	1979–82 (averages)				1985			
	Jan	*Feb*	*Mar*	*3 month Mean*	*Jan*	*Feb*	*Mar*	*3 month Mean*
Average daily min	−4.8	−6.0	−5.5	−5.4	−6.5	−5.4	−5.7	−5.9
Mean	−2.7	−4.5	−3.8	−3.7	−5.1	−3.1	−3.9	−4.0
Average daily max	−0.3	−2.5	−1.5	−1.4	−3.6	−1.0	−2.1	−2.2

(*Sources:* Heriot-Watt University, Dept of Physics and Meteorological Office, Edinburgh)

Table 2 gives some key comparative statistics from the Cairn Gorm AWS at 1,245 metres. Mean and *average* daily minimum temperatures are considerably lower than those at sea level, but the *absolute* range of temperatures is greater in the glen bottoms owing to the inversion phenomenon. Comparing the 1985 data to that for 1979–82, whilst January was significantly colder than usual, it is notable that February was in fact warmer than average in reversal of the sea-level pattern, for which difference inversions are again responsible.

Precipitation

Within the general paucity of snow and rainfall during the winter season there were significant regional variations, which directly impinged on the route and progress of the expedition, and are well shown by the Braemar–Onich data in Table 3. Most notably, January's 'drought' was confined to the western half of the country whilst the Cairngorms and Grampians experienced above-average precipitation (almost entirely as snow) under the continual attention of weak fronts advancing from the North Sea. Reversing the normal pattern, the west side was effectively in the 'rain shadow' of the eastern hills which soaked up most of the month's limited available moisture.

Table 3 Rainfall Totals (mm)

		Braemar	Onich
Dec	1984	77	322
	1951–80 average	96	238
	% of average	80%	135%
Jan	1985	117	72
	1951–80 average	93	200
	% of average	126%	36%
Feb	1985	19	99
	1951–80 average	59	132
	% of average	32%	75%
Mar	1985	60	107
	1951–80 average	59	152
	% of average	102%	70%
4 month totals 1984/85		273	600
	1951–80 average	307	722
	% of average	89%	83%

(*Source:* Meteorological Office, Edinburgh)

In February, the persistence of dry anticyclonic conditions produced exceptionally low precipitation in the east, whereas the only rain-bearing air was borne during the brief periods of Atlantic influence and so affected only the west coast.

In close contact with these variations, and applying our chosen flexibility of movement, we therefore stayed in the west for most of January, then captured the eastern hills during their own drought in February. Here our mobile tactics were applied to the greatest effect, and one can envisage the problems of a continuous winter Munros' journey on a predetermined route when such sly manoeuvres would be unavailable.

The 1984–85 experience shows how judicious the winter walker and climber needs to be in his selection of venue. The West Highlands provided superb hard walking conditions for most of January, while the Cairngorms were repeatedly being sprinkled with difficult fresh snow. The ice climber however has different requirements. Owing to the absence of drainage on the cliffs, there were poor pickings in the west in January, and he would have fared better in the east where at least there was plenty of powder snow on the faces.

The regional detail should not colour the basic fact that this was one of the most snowless winters on record. Much of the precipitation that did fall came as rain at all levels, eg late December, 8–9 March, and 23 February when Onich had its highest day's total in the season, of 37.2mm.

The *type* of precipitation on the mountain tops is a particular determinant of the climbing conditions, and almost infinite gradations can be observed when temperatures are around zero. Table 4 shows an attempted classification of the types I witnessed at the 3,000 foot level.

Table 4 Types of Precipitation during Winter 1984/85

Dominant Form at 3,000ft	Days	
Drizzle	5	
Rain	8	
Sleet	5	
Hail	3	+2 to −2°C
Contact freezing (rime ice)	3	air temperature
Freezing rain	2	
Wet snow	7	
Wind-driven snow (ie, pulverised)	5	
Light dry snow	<u>12</u>	
Total numbers of days with precipitation	50	

Freezing rain creates a special hazard to the mountaineer. It occurs when supercooled water droplets freeze on impact with the ground surface, producing sheet ice. By comparison, rime ice commonly forms on an influx of warm moist air after a prolonged period of frost.

Cloud Cover

Anticyclonic conditions are not always clear, and can produce either valley fogs associated with inversions or a high level 'stratocumulus' type of cloud which rarely drops below the summits and gives those raw leaden days of which we had several in January; but the thick low cloud associated with the moist Atlantic depressions was much less conspicuous than usual in the 1984/85 season.

Cloud cover is of course one of the most crucial factors to the safety and especially the enjoyment of mountaineers, and whilst the cloudbase is predicted in the specialist forecasts, there are no records of visibility levels on the summits. Table 5 provides a summary of my own observations during the 83 days (with estimates for the rest days!) .

Table 5 Cloud Cover and Visibility during the 1984/85 Winter

Avge Daytime Cloudbase (Height in metres)	Days	Min Visibility at 3,000ft (Distance in metres)	Days
0–300	2	Less than 25	10*
300–600	21	25–50	10
600–900	25	50–100	20
900–1200	11	100–200	14
Cloud above 1200	8	Clear	29
Sky clear	16		

(* Including 7 'white outs' with nil visibility)
NB Total no of Munros which gave me a view – 172 (62%)

Wind

The climber must be aware of the impact on human movement of different windspeeds before any proper perspective can be gained of this crucial factor. Any wind in excess of 30mph (26 knots or Force 6) can exert a chilling effect of around 20°C on a moving walker and will palpably slow his progress. At Gale Force 8 (39–46mph) progress is severely impeded (energy output probably at least trebled); at Force 10 (55–63mph) walking becomes difficult in itself; and at Force 12 (over 73mph) balance and breathing are affected, and crawling is the most efficient mode of travel. However, a clear distinction must be made between the velocity of the maximum *gusts,* and the *average* windspeed encountered on the summits. Generally gusts are around 25% greater than the mean speed, but occasionally can be double the average velocity. Our experience on the Feshie Hills on 9–10 February typifies the scenario when a Force 10 *average* gale is in flow struggling gamely in the 'lulls', then crawling and clinging to axes in the gusts of 80mph. Gustiness can never be adequately forecast in official bulletins, being largely determined by local terrain, but should always be added to the climber's calculations to derive the likely windspeeds that will be met on the hill tops.

Autumn and winter are by far the windiest seasons on the Scottish mountains. Taking the 1979–82 Cairn Gorm AWS data, the *percentage* of hours in which at least one $2^1/_2$ minute period of gale-force winds was recorded was 30.8 in both autumn and winter, but only 13.2 and 9.5 in spring and summer respectively. It is also noticeable that the *relative* windiness at high compared to low altitudes is much greater in winter. The Cairn Gorm winter mean of 34.3mph is nearly three times greater than that for Kinloss on the Moray Firth, whereas the summer average is only double that at the sea-level station.

The ambient gradient of air pressure is the main determinant of mean windspeed, although the vertical boundaries between airmasses of significantly different temperature and moisture are major additional sources of atmospheric turbulence over and around hills. Thus, owing to the dominance of stable high-pressure systems, the 1984/85 season was relatively windless. The steep pressure drops and airmass mixing associated with the Atlantic depressions were generally absent, except at the beginning and end of the season, and for brief periods in late January and mid-February. At Kinloss the mean windspeed for the four winter months was only 80% of its average over the previous 22 years. Tiree on the West coast showed an even more striking lack of wind with only 4 days with gales in January and February compared to an average of 13 over the previous 10 years, which especially illustrates the absence of Atlantic storms. And whilst these sea-level stations do not in any way replicate the mountain-top conditions, my own observations as shown on Table 6 (overleaf) clearly confirm the conclusion.

The highest $2^1/_2$ minute mean on Cairn Gorm summit in 1984/85 was 106mph on 8 February when we turned back from the White Lady Shieling. This

*Table 6 Distribution of Maximum Windspeeds Experienced at 3,000ft during
1984/85 winter*

Maximum Daytime Windspeed *	Days
Gale, greater than 39mph	26
Strong, 29–38mph	11
Fresh, 19–28mph	17
Moderate, 9–18mph	11
Nil/light, 0–8mph	18

(*Max estimated speed sustained over a period of more than 10 minutes)
(NB The *expected* no of days with significant gales was 42, see Ch 1)

Fig 1 Directional distribution (in percentages) of Scotland's winter winds (*source:*
Meteorological Office, Edinburgh)

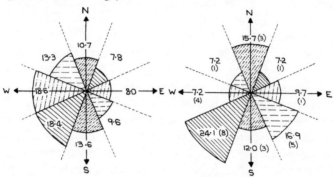

Stornoway: average free air wind directions; December–March 1961–70

Observed wind directions on Munro
summits; 1984/85 winter (83 days). Days
with gales in brackets

compares to an all-time maximum $2^{1}/_{2}$ minute mean of 124mph in January
1983, and a single-gust maximum of 148mph in December 1978.
Unfortunately the instruments malfunctioned during the great blizzard of 21
January 1984 and so no reliable data was obtained.

The analysis of the *directional distribution* of each day's wind in Fig 1 provides
a good basis for assessing the prevalent climatic influences on Scotland's winter
conditions. Whilst the most likely air stream is from the south-west quarter,
the average data for Stornoway on the Outer Hebrides shows that the winds
(and gales) can blow from any direction with appreciable frequency, and
indeed these readings are obviously biased towards the Westerlies compared
to the norms experienced in the Central or Eastern Highlands. However the
east and south-east winds are only significantly influential in January and
February when continental airmasses commonly take command of the weather.

The comparison of my own summit observations illustrates the abnormal
switch away from the westerly airflow during the 1984/85 season. The
climber might also note that my 26 'days with gales' were spread around all
points of the compass, but with 8 Sou'Westers and 5 Sou'Easters as the
greatest individual scores.

Weather Maps and Mountain Climate

It is the synoptic weather chart which gives the climber the greatest scope for predicting the *range* of possibilities in hill conditions, provided the necessary degree of basic meteorological knowledge is possessed.

A comparison of four of the widely differing weather situations we encountered during the 1984–5 season with the forecast weather charts for those days might help to illustrate some of the rules and guidelines which can be applied in their interpretation.

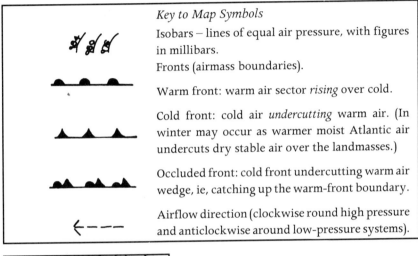

Key to Map Symbols

Isobars – lines of equal air pressure, with figures in millibars.

Fronts (airmass boundaries).

Warm front: warm air sector *rising* over cold.

Cold front: cold air *undercutting* warm air. (In winter may occur as warmer moist Atlantic air undercuts dry stable air over the landmasses.)

Occluded front: cold front undercutting warm air wedge, ie, catching up the warm-front boundary.

Airflow direction (clockwise round high pressure and anticlockwise around low-pressure systems).

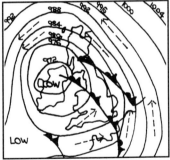

Noon, 21 Jan, 1985 – The Start of the Big Blizzard
Deep depression crossing from SW to NE of Scotland; advancing front drawing moist Atlantic air over colder continental airmasses and winding round the depression centre to form a strong easterly air stream over Scotland.
Mountain Weather Strong E Wind, temperature rising, thick cloud above 300 metres, heavy snowfall from mid-morning onwards, freezing level 400 metres, visibility less than 25 metres in blizzard.

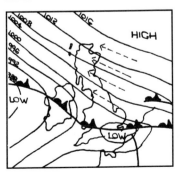

Noon, 9 Feb, 1985 – The Cairngorm Windstorm
Trough of low pressure across SW Britain blocked against Scandinavian anticyclone; steep pressure gradient producing strong continental airstream across Scotland; heavy snowfall confined to airmass boundary over south of country.
Mountain Weather Gale from SE up to Force 12 on summits; upper sky clear but storm shroud on tops fuelled by spindrift and scattered shower clouds blown in off North Sea; freezing all levels; 'white-out' conditions; moderate drifting and windslabbing on W slopes.

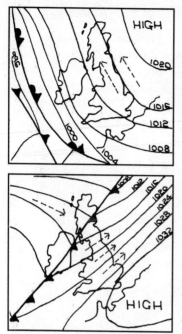

Noon, 12 Feb, 1985 – Mid-Month Freeze-up
Atlantic trough repelled by strengthening continental high, its associated depression forced northwards in mid-Atlantic and pressure gradient released. Very cold, dry but gentle SE airflow established.
Mountain Weather Light to moderate SE breeze, bitterly cold, summit temperatures about −5°C. Clear and dry; some high-level strato cloud, snow loose and unaltered on tops, windslab on drifted lee slopes.

Noon, 19 Feb, 1985 – The Storm that Faltered Cold front of moist Atlantic air undercutting the stable anticyclone from the NW; heavy cloud formation as moist air condenses on contact with colder dry air mass; *but* front pinned back by dominant 'high' – significant rain only on W side of country.
Mountain Weather (in Cairngorms) Gale from S and SW on tops, dense cloud above 500 metres; 'whiteout' on summits, light snow-fall with moderate drifting; freezing level rising to 600 metres briefly; clearing and calmer in evening as 'high' regains command and pressure gradient drops.

Snow Conditions and Avalanche Risk

The *freezing level* bears the greatest influence on the snow conditions on the mountains, and Fig 2 gives the trace of the estimated shade daytime levels observed throughout the Munros' expedition. However the plot does not show the variation in the freezing heights between night and day which crucially determines the range of altitudes at which good climbing conditions might develop. For instance, a diurnal range of 600–900 metres will ensure consolidation of snow and build-up of ice at intermediate altitudes, but above 900 metres where there is no thawing at any time, the snow will remain loose, unaltered and unsatisfactory.

The recent history of the freezing levels also counts significantly in the evolution of conditions. The widespread freeze which followed the 21–22 January blizzard prevented any consolidation of the new snow. Deep drifts hindered travel, and the lee-slope windslabs lay unaltered, forming a suspended avalanche risk for several days. Conversely, the freeze-up of early January in the west succeeded a warm and wet late December so producing hard ice, frozen ground, and dependable snow.

In general, the 1984/85 winter gave long stable periods of frost in which snow and avalanche prediction was fairly simple. The greater problem comes when the freezing level yo-yos up and down and is accompanied by an assortment of precipitation under the attention of successive frontal passages. As Fig 2 shows, this only occurred in late December, at which time there was

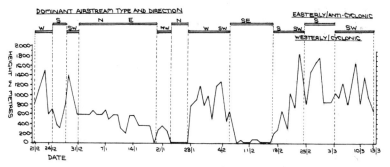
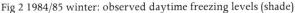

Fig 2 1984/85 winter: observed daytime freezing levels (shade)

insufficient build-up of snow to create any complexity of conditions or avalanche risk. Indeed, avalanche danger remained minimal for a large proportion of the season, and yet, for brief but crucial periods, the required predisposing factors combined to create a severe risk (as we discovered!). In fact, for 61 out of our 83 days on the Munros, I perceived that the avalanche risk in the high corries would have been minimal or weak, but there were four spells when the danger rose sharply, as shown below.

22–27 January

Heavy initial snowfall (at least 30cm at all levels).

Strong winds from E, N, and NW causing severe drifting on several slope aspects.

Persistent sub-zero temperatures preventing any breakdown or bonding of the lee-slope windslabs.

Danger An acute windslab danger thus persisted for 5 days requiring an external trigger. During the blizzard, accumulations were sufficiently heavy to cause natural avalanches of new snow, but on a modest scale.

8–12 February

Continuous SE gales packing all loose snow onto NW slopes.

Rapid freeze-up after mild spell at start of month – all old snow frozen hard, providing a perfect sliding surface for the new windslabs.

Sub-zero temperatures sustained throughout the period (–10.5°C on Cairngorm summit 8 Feb).

Danger Windslab risk but limited owing to absence of recent snowfall; depths of slabs never greater than 1 metre except on most sheltered corrie slopes.

28–29 January/23–24 February

Extremely rapid thaw (overnight rise in freezing level from 0 to 900 metres).

Deep unconsolidated existing snow cover in the case of 28–29 Jan.

Very heavy rainfall in the case of 23–24 Feb.

Danger Wet snow avalanche danger during melt and particularly a risk of cornice collapse; possible slides under the lubrication of running water at the base of the snow cover especially in the case of 23–24 Feb.

NB see Bibliography for other books on mountain weather and avalanches.

MUNRO MARATHONS: RUNS AND WALKS

Since Hamish Brown made the first continuous journey over all the Munros in 1974, there have been many remarkable Munro marathons, but very few have received significant media attention. Most mountain-marathoners are modest characters who have never sought personal fame and fortune from their endeavours. They have usually recorded their achievements, but have rarely publicised them.

This history aims to set down the most important of these, drawing together the widely scattered records of past deeds to give as accurate and objective a record as possible. I have been forced to be selective and, inevitably, I will have missed some expeditions that would have been worthy of inclusion. So at the outset, I apologise to those whose efforts I have overlooked.

The history is grouped into three sections:
• The Munros: Complete or Continuous Journeys
• The 24-Hour Munros' Challenge
• Other Munro Rounds

Many readers may regard these record-making traverses as dour and soulless undertakings, and may think that their protagonists lack a proper aesthetic appreciation of the mountains. In nearly every case the opposite is true. To sustain a gruelling physical effort in the hills over a continuous 24-hour run or a 3-month expedition requires the utmost enthusiasm and passion for the mountain environment. From my personal experience I know that I could not have sustained my own winter effort without continuous inspiration from the hills.

Furthermore, to set oneself a target against the clock creates the potential for the most adventurous and exciting mountain escapades. Think of Charlie Ramsey's headlong dash down Ben Nevis to complete his round within 24 hours, or else the nightmare of a mid-summer blizzard endured by Adrian Belton on the Ossian hills on his 24-hour record attempt. Many have been epic battles of courage and willpower to rank with any in the wider field of mountaineering.

Finally, although my list focuses on the achievements of the last twenty-five years, let no one assume that mountain marathons are a recent invention. Such early luminaries of Scottish mountaineering as Willie Naismith and Sir Hugh Munro himself were great enthusiasts of extended excursions in the hills. Typical of such early 'stravaigs' in the hills was the circuit of all 12 tops on the upper Tilt and Shee hills by D. H. Menzies and W. M. Wilson in 1909, a mere 56 miles with 11,000ft of ascent in a push of $29\frac{1}{2}$ hours. The 'marathon game' has a long pedigree as well as an exciting future.

The Munros: Complete or Continuous Journeys

1967 The Ripleys' Attempt

Brian and Alan Ripley; 13 August–10 November; abandoned on Beinn Dorain after 230 Munros, 1,325 miles and 337,850ft of ascent. A bold attempt on a hitherto unspoken challenge by an English team; plagued by midges, access problems during the stalking season and supply difficulties; finally defeated by progressive exhaustion and appalling weather. The Ripleys began with the goal of a self-propelled journey but hitched some lifts in the latter stages. If only they had gone in the drier spring – no subsequent attempt has made the mistake of starting so late.

1974 'Hamish's Mountain Walk'

Hamish M. Brown; 4 April–24 July; 112 days; the *first* continuous round, self-propelled save for the Skye and Mull ferries; 1,639 miles (of which c150 were on bicycle) and 449,000ft of ascent; started Ben More, Mull and finished on Ben Hope. Fully documented in *Hamish's Mountain Walk*, now a classic. A solo journey save for 12 days; intricately planned and executed, using expert knowledge, food dumps and regular support rendezvous; Hamish Brown was already the most prolific Munroist ever with three completions before his continuous walk (by 1996 he had done the Munros seven times!).

1982 The First Lady

Kathy Murgatroyd aged 34 from the New Forest; 1 May–11 September; 134 days, 2,250 miles (including 1,000 by bicycle) and 460,000ft of ascent; started Ben More, Mull and finished on Sgurr Mhic Choinnich, Skye. The second continuous round with similar tactics to Hamish Brown, but executed in more modular style (ie cycling to a base and climbing all surrounding Munros from a fixed camp) and without Hamish's vast prior experience (Kathy had done only 154 Munros before this journey); despite regular support from boyfriend 196 summits were climbed solo.

1984 Britain's Three Thousanders

George Keeping of Preston; 14 April–27 August; 136 days; 1,784 miles and 464,000ft of ascent; the third continuous round and the first without the use of a bicycle; walk extended by a further 29 days to include the English and Welsh 3,000ft summits; started Ben Klibreck, finished Ben Chonzie; very little prior Munro-bagging experience; accompanied for around half of the walk; helped by very dry weather.

1984 The Mainland Munros

Rick Ansell of Hertfordshire; 3 May–10 August; 100 days; in Rick's own words: 'the mainland Munros in one bash, using no support, no bicycles, canoes or food parcels'; started Ben Lomond, finished Ben Hope. As to why he omitted the islands: 'The ferries would have spoilt the purity of the walk, which is a good excuse for not feeling competent to solo the Skye Ridge!' Rick claims the driest-ever Munros round, with only four soakings!

1984–5 The Winter Munros

Martin Moran, supported by his wife Joy; 83 days; 21 December–13 March; use of motorised transport to move between the mountains enabled a fast completion, additionally helped by a dry cold winter. To date this is the only completion in a single winter. The ultimate Munros' challenge remains a continuous winter round without motor transport – no takers so far!

1985–6 'Climb Every Mountain' – the Munros and Corbetts

Craig Caldwell; 16 February 1985–27 February 1986; 377 days; 4,152 miles cycled, 3,030 miles walked with 828,000ft of ascent; the addition of the 221 Corbetts (Scottish mountains between 2,500 and 3,000ft in height with 500ft of reascent on all sides) trebled the duration of the Munros traverse and necessitated visits to four different islands and the Southern Uplands. Craig endured the wettest summer since 1897 during his journey, which far surpasses anything done before or since in scale and duration.

1988 A Fast Completion

Mark Elsegood of Stockport; 22 May–26 July; all the Munros in 66 days; 1,054 miles and 411,250ft of ascent; using a car to move between the mountains; a significant reduction in the time for fastest completion and the first to employ the style and tactics of lightweight fell-running.

1989 The Munros by Mountain Bike

Paul Tattersall of Wigan; 81 days; 27 April–16 July; a continuous journey, riding or carrying a 35lb mountain bike up every peak; mountain-biking on fragile mountain terrain was rightly criticised at the time, but this should not obscure a remarkable feat of strength and endurance. Paul's round included a 17-hour traverse of the Cuillin Ridge with the bike dismantled and strapped to his back, prompting the comment from Hamish Brown: 'Anyone who takes a mountain bike up the Cuillin needs a psychiatrist.' Paul had only climbed his first Munro a year before his continuous round.

1990 Running High – the 3,000ft Mountains of the British Isles

Hugh Reynolds of Sedbergh, Cumbria, supported by his wife Pauline and family; a continuous journey entirely on foot; climbing the Munros in 67 days and then continuing over the '3,000ers' of England, Wales and Ireland to finish a superb grand slam in 97 days; started 19 April on Ben Hope and finished on Brandon Mountain 25 July; the Scottish part of the trip was completely self-propelled – Hugh sailed a yacht to Mull and rowed to Skye. He only added on the hills of Ireland as an afterthought because he was enjoying himself so much and didn't want to finish (to do this he had to take the ferry from Holyhead to Dublin). Hugh applied his experience as one of Britain's top fell and marathon runners to sustain 25 miles a day on road sections. His many pacers marvelled at his capacity to eat 5,000–6,000 calories a day – in fact Hugh *put on* half a stone in weight from the start to finish of the journey.

1992 The Great Munro Challenge

Rory Gibson and Andrew Johnston; the fastest-ever continuous Munros journey, 51 days and 10 hours; 1,400 miles (including 490 on road and mountain bike) and 400,000ft of ascent; continuous back-up support to change kit and keep moving. One highlight was a swim across Loch Lomond. Blessed by excellent weather until the last three weeks when gales and rain swept the North-West and forced them off their 50-day schedule. Although they believed the 50-day barrier could be broken, the record-breaking 'game' will henceforth be the preserve of highly-trained endurance athletes with efficient back-up organisation and will require considerable luck with the weather. Gone are the days of lonely unsupported epics in the style of the Ripleys.

1994 Cudahy's Round

Mike Cudahy, a legend in the world of endurance running and the first person to run the Pennine Way in under three days, used the free time offered by retirement to run the Munros in 66 days, one day faster than Hugh Symonds. This is the fastest completion of the Munros on foot, although Cudahy used the Mull and Skye ferries.

1996 The Munros and Tops

Chris Townsend; all the Munros and subsidiary Tops are listed in *Munro's Tables* (517 summits in all) in a continuous journey on foot; 118 days; 18 May–12 September; 1,700 miles and 575,000ft of ascent, carrying an average pack of 30lb, camping and walking solo throughout, with resupply from his girlfriend Denise Thorn and posted food parcels. A *tour de force* by Britain's most experienced long-distance back-packer. This leaves a continuous round of Munros, Tops and Corbetts in one go as Scotland's ultimate mountain marathon. My knees are hurting just writing about it!

The 24-Hour Munros' Challenge

1964 Tranter's Round

The circuit of the 19 Munros of Glen Nevis by Philip Tranter in 23 hours in June 1964 created *the* classic one-day Munros' round. Traversing the Ben Nevis–Grey Corries and Mamores ranges the route covers 35 miles with 20,000ft of ascent. Tranter was himself a double Munroist and one of Scotland's most enthusiastic pioneers before his untimely death in a car crash in 1966.

1983   3 June Martin Hudson of Keswick Athletic Club made a solo unsupported traverse of Tranter's route in 13hr 54min.

1990   28 May Mark McDermott, holder of the Lakeland 24-hour peaks record, completed the route, again solo and unsupported, in 12hr 50min, creating the current record.

1977 The Glen Shiel Circuit

The ridges of Glen Shiel and Loch Cluanie contain 20 Munros, a greater concentration than those around Glen Nevis. On 14–15 July 1977, Blyth Wright, who had accompanied Tranter for much of his Glen Nevis round 13 years earlier, kept his friend's spirit alive by attempting the Shiel round. He managed 17 of the 20 summits in a time of 23½hr, missing out Tigh Mor na Seilge, Sgurr na Sgine and The Saddle. This was done in plastic climbing boots with a half-hour break for a couple of pints of shandy at Cluanie Inn. There are no records of anyone completing the Glen Shiel circuit, save for John Broxap in 1988 (see below).

Ramsay's Round

The extension of Tranter's route to incorporate five loch Treig Munros (Beinn na Lap, Chno Dearg, Stob Coire Sgriodain, Stob a'Choire Mheadhoin and Stob Coire Easain) to make a '24 Munros in 24 hours' challenge and thus create Scotland's definitive one-day round. At 58 miles with 28,000ft of ascent it is directly comparable to Lakeland's Bob Graham Round, but traverses much rougher, steeper and more remote terrain.

1978   8–9 July Charlie Ramsay of Edinburgh, who devised the extended round and who had done 1,600 miles with 270,000ft of climbing during six months' training for his attempt, just pipped the 24-hour barrier by two minutes. His companion, Bobby Shields, had to retire after two-thirds of the run. They traversed the Mamores first, then Ramsay lost the route twice in mist on the Grey Corries and fund that he had only 35 minutes to get from the summit of Ben Nevis down to his starting point at Glen Nevis Youth Hostel. In the final dash none of his pacers could keep up with him!

  Ramsay's Round had been repeated inside 24 hours 16 times by the end of 1996. Most notable of these were:

1989 15 July Helen Diamantides completed the round with Mark Rigby in 21hr 24min setting the woman's record.

1989 2 August Adrian Belton created a fine record of 18hr 23min.

1990 27 May Bob Berzins did the round solo and unsupported in 21hr 55min.

1990 13 July Mike Hartley completed the route in 21hr 14min, but instead of going to bed he was driven down to the Lake District where he did the Bob Graham Round in 21hr 48min. Still not content, he was immediately shipped down to Wales where he did the Paddy Buckley Round in 33hr 30min, so completing the staggering achievement of doing Britain's three definitive 24-hour rounds in 3½ days.

1987 The Solo Unsupported Record – Ramsay's Extension

Martin Stone; 25–26 June; running entirely solo and unsupported with his food supplies stuffed into bum bags and pocket pouches, Martin added the Ossian hills of Sgor Gaibhre and Carn Dearg on to Ramsay's Round, climbing 26 Munros in a round trip from Glen Nevis Youth Hostel in 23hr 24min; 70

miles with 31,000ft of ascent; the extra effort and psychological challenge of a purely solo run are enormous, and this remains the 24-hour Munro record for a self-supported run.

1988 The Broxap Round – Shiel, Cluanie and Affric
John Broxap of Keswick; 25–26 June; 28 Munros, extending the Glen Shiel–Cluanie circuit to include all the Munros of Glen Affric except Toll a'Choinich and Toll Creagach, in 23hr 20min; 77½ miles with 33,300ft of ascent; paced and supported (although none of his helpers could keep up with him!), and sustained by a diet of tinned peaches, Weetabix and squashed bananas. A magnificent run, taking the 24-hour record to a completely new area. Broxap emigrated to Australia a day after the run (he is now back in Britain).

1991 Belton's Twenty-Eight
Adrian Belton; 1–2 June; 28 Munros in 23hr 57min, adding three Munros of the Ossian Aonach Beag group to Martin Stone's round but missing out Beinn na Lap; 75 miles with 34,000ft of ascent. Three days before the attempt Belton was in Fort William's hospital with a badly gashed and bruised elbow sustained in training. His aim was an outright record of 29 or 30 Munros in a day, and this was his third attempt on the round. Luck deserted him again when he hit a snowstorm on the Corrour hills at midnight. By curtailing his route, he just made it back to his starting point at Fersit Dam within 24 hours.

It is testimony to the magnitude of these achievements that no one is known to have attempted the 24-hour record since 1991, although the possibility exists to extend the number of summits to 30 in both Lochaber and Affric.

Other Munro Rounds
The Cuillin Ridge of Skye
Gars-bheinn to Sgurr nan Gillean; 11 Munros, 8 miles and 7,000ft of ascent with rock climbing up to Severe standard; the finest mountaineering expedition in the British Isles first completed by Leslie Shadbolt and A. McLaren in 1911 in 12hr 20min and progressively reduced to an unofficial record of 6hr 45min by D. Stewart. Traversed against the clock, the Ridge is a unique challenge, combining running and climbing skills with more than a dash of danger. *1966* The renowned fell-runner, climber and comedian, Eric Beard, did the Ridge solo in 4hr 9min. However, he by-passed the Inaccessible Pinnacle and a rope had been fixed for him at the T–D Gap.
1984   7 May Andy Hyslop of Ambleside followed the complete definitive traverse, taking in all 11 Munros and soloing all the climbing difficulties (including the T–D Gap and Bhaisteir Tooth) in 4hr 4min; two support points en route.

1986   12 August Del Davies and Paul Stott of Eyri Harriers completed the Hyslop route in 3hr 50min, breaking the psychological barrier of 4hr and running unsupported.

1990   2 June Martin Moran made a solo unsupported traverse of the Hyslop route in 3hr 33min, his routefinding benefiting from his having guided the Ridge previously over a dozen times.

1994   25 May/7 August Andy Hyslop returned for two further record attempts, both solo. On the first he equalled the record, and on the second trimmed a minute off the time to create a new mark of 3hr 32min. The risks of going much faster may deter further attempts, although there are definitely several minutes to be saved!

The Cairngorm Four-Thousanders

Braeriach, Cairn Toul, Ben Macdui and Cairn Gorm; starting and finishing at Glenmore Lodge; 25 miles and 8,000ft of ascent. Perhaps more popular as a winter ski tour, but summer records have been set by Eric Beard in 1967 (4hr 41min) and Mel Edwards in 1979 (4hr 34min).

The Six Cairngorm Tops

The four-thousanders plus Ben Avon and Beinn a'Bhuird; the definitive Cairngorm expedition, traditionally done east–west starting at Loch Builg; 28 miles and 9,000ft of ascent; first recorded in 1908 in a time of 19hr; most notably, completed in 9hr 34min in 1968 by Prof V. C. Wyn-Harris, then in his sixties!

Done as a round trip, starting and finishing at Glenmore Lodge, in 1985 by Dave Armitage, Mel Edwards and Phil Kammer in a time of 11hr 39min; 39 miles with 12,500ft of ascent. This is undoubtedly the premier Scottish ski tour, being often in condition on account of its high altitude. It was first recorded as such by Adam Watson in April 1962 who did the route solo in 16 hours starting from Invercauld and finishing at Derry Lodge. Watson used wooden langlauf skis from Lapland, skied 34 of the 38 miles and was fuelled by six tins of fruit.

The Glencoe Munros

Bidean nam Bian, Buachaille Etive Beag, Buachaille Etive Mor, Am Bodach, Sgurr nam Fiannaidh; starting and finishing from Clachaig Inn; 19 miles with 12,750ft of ascent; done in 7hr 5min on 31 May 1980 by Bobby Shields of Lochaber Athletic Club.

Tour of the Mamores

All 11 Munros and 6 tops of the Mamores in a round trip from Glen Nevis; 21 miles with 10,000ft of ascent; it was done in 7hr 2min by Colin Donnelly on 1 July 1980.

The Torridon Hills

The 'big three' of Beinn Eighe, Liathach and Beinn Alligin offer a memorable one-day challenge. This was done end-to-end from Kinlochewe to Alligin car park following each main ridge in full in 6hr 55min by Martin Moran on 27 October 1985; 20 miles with 12,450ft ascent. Paul Potter later added Beinn Dearg to the trio of Munro mountains, and did the round trip of the four peaks from the Coire Dubh car park inside 10hr.

Scotland's 4,000ft Summits

Established as a long-distance walk by the Rucksack Club in 1954, linking the Cairngorm and Lochaber four-thousanders by a classic overland trek from Glen Feshie through the Ben Alder Forest to Glen Nevis; 85 miles with 17,000ft ascent; 8 full Munros (Aonach Mor at 3,999ft is included for safety's sake!). First attempted as a 24-hour run by veteran Lakeland fell-runner, Alan Heaton, in 1979.

In July 1980 Chris Dodd of Dark Peak Fell Runners broke the one-day barrier with a time of 23hr 14min from Glenmore Lodge to Glen Nevis Youth Hostel. The route was done solo and unsupported by Martin Stone on 4 July 1986 in a new record time of 21hr 39min.

Scotland Coast-to-Coast

For many years the object of an annual challenge hike organised by *The Great Outdoors* magazine. There are no pre-determined routes for this challenge save that the route finishes in the vicinity of Montrose on the east coast. A substantial number of Munros can be included en route.

In the summer of 1983, Ian Leighton and Robin Price did a 5-day crossing from Inverie in Knoydart to Montrose, climbing 18 Munros including the 8 four-thousanders, and running 230 miles with 35,000ft of climbing. They were almost entirely self-supported, living as vagabonds of the hills, with open bivouacs and a disgusting diet of Complan and powdered glucose diluted in stream water. Only on Lochnagar did their resolve waver. Feeling especially hungry they made a 10-mile detour for a fish supper at the Ballater 'chippie'. This sustained them for the night run of 40 miles to Montrose!

Many other 'big rounds' of Munros have been done over the years. Those recorded above are only the best-established as specific challenges. Strong walkers and fell-runners will be able to devise many other routes that will give the mountain days of a lifetime, whether or not the objective is to set or break records.

BIBLIOGRAPHY

With the continuing increase in public interest and participation in hill-walking and climbing, there has been a stream of guidebooks and narratives on the Munros in the last twelve years. The flow shows no sign of abating. You can buy Munro wallcharts and pocket diaries and they are now even available on CD Rom. I have listed texts which are primarily concerned with the Munros rather than general books on Scottish mountaineering.

Guidebooks
Munro's Tables Ed by D. A. Bearhop (Scottish Mountaineering Club; revised 1990) – the Munro-baggers 'bible'; with an excellent historical section and Gaelic glossary.

The Munros Ed by Donald Bennet (Scottish Mountaineering Club; revised edition 1991) – peak-by-peak guidebook with concise descriptions of the easiest route to each summit; a bestseller with over 40,000 hardback sales in the ten years since its first publication in 1985.

The High Mountains of Britain and Ireland: Vol 1 Irvine Butterfield (Diadem, 1986) – a guide to the 3,000ft mountains describing the best traverses of the main groups; beautifully illustrated. A condensed *Companion Volume* minus the photos is also available for use on the hills.

50 Best Routes on Scottish Mountains Ralph Storer (David & Charles, 1994)
50 More Routes on Scottish Mountains Ralph Storer (David & Charles, 1995)
Two volume version of *100 Best Routes on Scottish Mountains* first published in 1987; most of the routes include Munros.

100 Best Routes on Scottish Mountains Ralph Storer (Warner Books paperback, 1992)

The Munros Almanac Cameron McNeish (Neil Wilson Publishing, 1996) – pocket-size guide to each peak.

The Munros Cameron McNeish (Lomond Press, 1996) – new text in similar style to Butterfield's *High Mountains*; beautifully illustrated with Colin Baxter's photos and 3-D maps.

Narratives
Hamish's Mountain Walk Hamish Brown (Gollancz hardback, Granada paperback) – the story of the first continuous traverse and the springboard for all that followed; a delightful anecdotal companion to the Munros interwoven with their social and natural history.

Climb Every Mountain Craig Caldwell (McDonald hardback 1990, Sphere paperback 1991) – Craig's journey over all the Munros and Corbetts.